Fan Identities in the Furry Fandom

Fan Identities in the Furry Fandom

Jessica Ruth Austin

BLOOMSBURY ACADEMIC
LONDON • NEW YORK • OXFORD • NEW DELHI • SYDNEY

BLOOMSBURY ACADEMIC
Bloomsbury Publishing Inc
1385 Broadway, New York, NY 10018, USA
50 Bedford Square, London, WC1B 3DP, UK
29 Earlsfort Terrace, Dublin 2, Ireland

BLOOMSBURY, BLOOMSBURY ACADEMIC and the Diana logo are trademarks of
Bloomsbury Publishing Plc

First published in the United States of America 2021
This paperback edition published 2023

For legal purposes the Acknowledgements on p. vii constitute an extension
of this copyright page.

Cover design and illustration: Rebecca Heselton
Fur textures © Gooddenka/ThomasVogel/iStock

Bloomsbury Publishing Inc does not have any control over, or responsibility for, any
third-party websites referred to or in this book. All internet addresses given in this
book were correct at the time of going to press. The author and publisher regret any
inconvenience caused if addresses have changed or sites have ceased to exist, but can
accept no responsibility for any such changes.

Library of Congress Cataloging-in-Publication Data
Names: Austin, Jessica Ruth, author.
Title: Fan identities in the furry fandom / Jessica Ruth Austin.
Description: New York : Bloomsbury Academic, 2021. |
Includes bibliographical references and index.
Identifiers: LCCN 2021007989 (print) | LCCN 2021007990 (ebook) |
ISBN 9781501375439 (hardback) | ISBN 9781501375422 (ebook) |
ISBN 9781501375415 (pdf)
Subjects: LCSH: Furry fandom (Subculture) | Human-animal
relationships–Social aspects. | Costume–Social aspects. |
Subculture. Classification: LCC QL85 .A87 2021 (print) | LCC QL85 (ebook) |
DDC 591.5–dc23
LC record available at https://lccn.loc.gov/2021007989
LC ebook record available at https://lccn.loc.gov/2021007990

ISBN: HB: 978-1-5013-7543-9
PB: 978-1-5013-7540-8
ePDF: 978-1-5013-7541-5
eBook: 978-1-5013-7542-2

Typeset by Newgen KnowledgeWorks Pvt. Ltd., Chennai, India

To find out more about our authors and books visit www.bloomsbury.com
and sign up for our newsletters.

Contents

Acknowledgements

To my family and friends, thank you. Due to your immense support, you are off the hook for reading this book.

Introduction: The Furry Fandom

Furry fandom is a recent phenomenon, but anthropomorphism is an instinct hard-wired into the human mind: the desire to see animals on a more equal footing with people. It's existed since the beginning of time in prehistoric cave paintings, ancient gods and tribal rituals. It lives on today – not just in the sports mascots and cartoon characters we see everywhere, but in stage plays, art galleries, serious literature, performance art – and among furry fans who bring their make-believe characters to life digitally, on paper, or in the carefully crafted fursuits they wear to become the animals of their imagination.

– Strike (2017)

Who are the Furries?

The subject of this book centres on the members of the Furry Fandom, known colloquially as the Furries. There is currently little peer-reviewed research on the Furry Fandom outside of the research group, International Anthropomorphic Research Project (IARP), who have focused much of their research on the fandom. In their work they describe the group, and individuals within it, as the following:

A Furry is a person who identifies with the Furry Fandom culture. Furry Fandom is the collective name given to individuals who have a distinct interest in anthropomorphic animals such as cartoon characters. Many, but not all, Furries strongly identify with, or view themselves as, one (or more) species of animal other than human. Common Furry identities ('fursonas') are dragon, feline (cat, lion, tiger), and canine (wolf, fox, domestic dog) species. Some Furries create mixed species such as a 'folf' (fox and wolf) or 'cabbit' (cat and rabbit). Furries rarely, if ever, identify with a nonhuman primate species. Many Furries congregate in cyberspace, enjoy artwork depicting anthropomorphized animals, and attend Furry Fandom conventions. (Gerbasi et al. 2008, 198)

It can be difficult to pinpoint a year in which the Furry Fandom started due to the unusual nature of the fandom itself. Unlike other fandoms it is not based on a TV show or a film franchise. Whereas these types of fandoms are easy to historicize as you can pinpoint the *start*, such as when people watched the TV pilot for instance, there is no singular cultural touchstone for Furries. However, consensus among Furries themselves seems to suggest that the fandom started in the 1980s; despite not being based on any particular base media text. Furries who have been in the fandom since the 1980s often cite an increase in popularity and exposure beginning in the 1990s (Nyareon 2015, 7). There was, however, a small contingent of what would become part of the Furry Fandom in as early as April 1976. This coincided with the launch of *Vootie* 'The fanzine of the Furry Animal Liberation Front', which ran until February 1983 (Patten 2015, 36). However, the first specific Furry publication was not available until May 1987 and was named *FurVersion*, but this ceased distribution in November 1990 (ibid.). While the fandom has now spread around the globe, its earliest documentable origins are in the United States. Referring to himself as a prominent 'Furry historian', Fred Patten states his belief that the concept of 'Furry' originated in earnest from Steve Gallacci's *Albedo Anthropomorphics*. This comic strip was being sold at a US science fiction convention in 1980 (Patten 2012).

The internet has helped to facilitate the rapid and mass dissemination of artwork and fiction – previous hard copy magazines and fanzines were previously hard to find for those not already within the fandom. Technological advancements resulted in an increase in communication as Furries used internet services such as Skype to communicate with friends if they are unable to attend Fur Meets (Shoji 2015, 17). Since the 1990s Furry Fandom membership has continued to grow and now Furry conventions are held in several countries over the course of the year.

In the United States there are multiple conventions dedicated to those who are interested in anthropomorphics. Some of the largest conventions include the Midwest Furfest, which in 2017 hosted 8,771 attendees in Illinois and

Furry Weekend Atlanta which in 2017 hosted 5,193 attendees in Georgia. The United States still dominates in terms of attendance compared to the rest of the world, but numbers are increasing at conventions in other parts of the globe, most noticeably in Berlin, Germany. From humble beginnings with an attendance of nineteen people in June 1995, Eurofurence has continued to grow in attendance; in 2017, Eurofurence had 2,804 attendees, making it the largest and the longest running Furry convention outside of the United States.[1]

As with other fandoms, there have also been several prominent and popular members who have helped shape the fandom into what it is today. In 2008, a 'Furry Hall of Fame' was conceived by MiDFur chairman CynWolfe, and several prominent members of the fandom have since been inducted into it. Patten was inducted in 2011 for his work trying to chronicle the fandom history. Also among the inductees was Uncle Kage, who has chaired Anthrocon since 1999, and the Ranting Gryphon, who is an amateur comedian and performer who commonly makes appearances at Furry conventions. There are also several well-known publishers of Furry material, such as Howl Publications. Howl Publications is run by a Furry by the name of Thurston Howl; in 2015, Howl published an anthology with chapters written by prominent members of the fandom about important aspects of the fandom such as costuming and vernacular.

The description given of the Furries by Gerbasi et al. (2008) at the start of this chapter comes from their work titled *Furries from A–Z*, the first ever peer-reviewed study on Furries, which was conducted at a Furry convention in the United States. They looked to find common denominators (if any) of the 'stereotypical' identifiers of being a Furry compared to actual demographics of the Furry population. According to the IARP, an almost universal and identifiable part of being a Furry is the creation of a fursona.[2] This is a special character drawn by the Furry themselves or commissioned by an artist. The Furry can use this character to identify themselves as a Furry to others in real-life as well as in online spaces by using it as an avatar. These fursonas are comic/animated anthropomorphized animals and come in various colours, shapes and sizes while always being identifiable as a different species to our own. In fact, if you have ever seen a group of people wandering around in very colourful 'animal-looking' costumes, you have very likely just seen a Furry and simultaneously their fursona. This is because some Furries are able to make their drawn character into a suit which they can wear out and about. In recent years, it can be suggested that anthropomorphic and anime fandoms have been progressive in eschewing 'traditional' ascribed gender roles. When *My Little Pony* was rebooted to create a new show called *My Little Pony: Friendship Is Magic*, the show's creators were surprised to have found a huge following, not consisting of little girls for whom the show was intended, but men in their twenties (and beyond) as well.[3] Lauren Faust (who proposed the reboot to Hasbro) attended BronyCon as a guest speaker:

> 'I wanted a respectable show for girls,' Faust explains. 'Saying something is "for girls" or "girly" is usually equated with being not worthwhile, being stupid.' She wanted to change that, but she never expected she'd be so successful. 'I never dreamed adult men would be into the show,' she tells the crowd, 'because I didn't have any faith that you'd give it a try. Now I know better. It gives me the courage to continue.' (Wilson 2012)

Christopher Bell noted that when 'fan-boys attach themselves to cultural properties which were *not intended* for them, it can be easy to write the fandom off as a sort of ironic statement. But Bronies exhibit much of what could be thought of as *neo-sincerity*' (Bell 2013, 9; emphasis in original). Bell believes that the Bronies genuinely enjoy the show, rather than using the show as a platform for trolling or for ironic purposes. There is also a similar notion for the Furries interviewed for this book who often feel that they can be childish within the fandom as they are not 'allowed' to do this in the real world. This can be attributed to 'childishness' not conforming to traditional male gender stereotypes.

The IARP regard Furries' use of fursonas as a process of self-authentication, using the species of their chosen fursona to personify certain personality traits that the Furry had, or wished to be perceived as having (Gerbasi et al. 2008, 239). Their research suggests it is uncommon for a Furry to have more than two fursonas at one given time, though this can be subject to change based on species, characteristics and personality (Plante et al. 2015, 13). In social sciences, the concept of authenticity can be argued as when 'one is true to one's self' and thus authenticity is a 'self-reflective and emotional experience' (Vannini and Franzese 2008, 1621). In the study of Gerbasi et al., the way that Furries use their fursonas is then a way to experience authenticity in a way that they cannot experience using their own personality or indeed body, in their real lives; the fursona becomes a conduit. There are varying lengths to which Furries self-identify with their fursona, with some Furries considering themselves as not wholly human, that is, 'a person who is, feels, or believes he/she is in part or whole (non-physically) one or more non-human animals on an integral, personal level' (Grivell et al. 2014, 115). One such subgroup of the Furry Fandom is a group known as Therians. Some Furries can be Therian in that they also identify as not wholly human. But not all Furries are Therians as they do consider themselves human, which is why in this book they are considered a separate group. In addition, there are Furries who would be considered as Therians under the definition but would not want to identify as such.

There is some conflict within the Therian subgroup as in what way identification with the animal is socially acceptable. This issue is seen between Therians who believe they can 'shift' into an animal and Therians who identify as not wholly human on a spiritual or psychological level. Some Therian online forums ban posts expressing the belief in 'p-shifting' (physical shifting) from animal to human, for example, in lycanthropy (Robertson 2012, 270). The reason why this tension occurs is because Therians who may only identify with the animal spiritually, think that the Therians who truly believe they can change into an animal give the group a bad name. This is seen in the wider Furry Fandom as well; Furries who consider the fandom as just a hobby rather than an identity/or similar to Therianthropy are at odds as they believe those who are 'heavily identified' cause the whole group to be stigmatized by the wider society.

The Furry Fandom is overwhelmingly under the age of 25 with the IARP finding that nearly 75 per cent of self-described Furries are under this age (Plante et al. 2016, 4). This has been the case for many years with Furry fan–run AdjectiveSpecies.com polling for the last several years showing a median age of 19 years.[4] Although there is nothing inherently wrong with fandoms being 'young', there has been evidence in other studies where 'there is an implication that there are fan spaces in which age is problematic' (McCudden 2011, 103). There are examples in other fandoms where age can become more of an issue than it appears in the Furry Fandom such as noted by Matt Hills in the *Doctor Who* fandom (Hills 2014). In my research, however, there was far more concern about inappropriate interactions between older fans and younger ones. There are legitimate concerns as to why interacting with Furries under the age of 18 can cause potential issues (e.g. fandoms can sometimes be concerned about distribution of erotica). Although some fandoms worry about older participants being pushed out. This is uncommon within the Furry Fandom as many older Furries are highly respected. They are often viewed as pioneers within the fandom; it was the older fans who started the conventions that have become popular today. In the glossary provided at the end of this book, 'grey muzzle' is used as an affectionate term for older Furries rather than a derogatory one.

The Furry Fandom has traditionally been overwhelmingly white as well. A poll on AdjectiveSpecies.com has seen the white ethnicity sitting around 89 per cent of all Furries polled for the past seven years.[5] The IARP have repeatedly seen the white ethnicity over-represented in their studies as well; their research has seen a slightly lower proportion of those who self-identify as white 'with 15–20% of Furries identifying as an ethic minority' (Plante et al. 2016, 7). Although intra-fandom racism could be a cause for a dominant white demographic, there are few studies on this within the Furry Fandom context, and so to theorize on this would only be conjecture. Despite this, it is important to recognize research on ethnicity within other fandoms that may be applicable to the Furry Fandom when it comes to future study. In fan studies it is often noted that the default stereotype for a fan, and usually a fan boy, is

> white, middle-class, male, heterosexual (with perhaps an overlay or geek or nerd identity, identities that are simultaneously embedded in emphasized whiteness, and increasingly certain kinds of class privilege, often displayed by access to higher education, particularly in scientific and technical fields). (Gatson and Reid 2012)

Academics have argued that many fandoms are predominantly white in ethnicity due to many fandoms being a product of capitalism where white men control the product (Stanfill and Condis 2014). Mel Stanfill had also argued that much discourse in fandom studies has focused on 'whiteness' in that fans have been constructed as white, heterosexual males (2011, 2018).

In current studies, the Furry Fandom is presented as overwhelmingly male in gender, with my research for this book totalling 90 per cent male respondents. This is consistent with the findings by the IARP (Gerbasi et al. 2008; Plante et al. 2016, 10). This is also comparable to other related fandoms such as anime fandoms, which tend to be predominantly male (ibid.). Although there is data on the male members of the Furry Fandom, there is little data on why women are not more involved in the fandom. Some academics have argued that the over-representation of males within fandoms in general has been due to misogynistic practices. Suzanne Scott discusses the discourse of the 'fan-boy' (Scott 2012) who can become angry and aggressive towards anyone who is deemed as not suitable for the fandom. However, IARP research suggests that female Furries who are present are less likely to 'feel a sense of fandom'. These women were more likely to want to retain non-Furry culture, in addition to Furry culture, but were unable to pinpoint exactly why this was (IARP 2017).

In several studies by the IARP it has been found that there is a plethora of sexualities in the Furry Fandom and it is one of the few fandoms which is not predominantly heterosexual (Gerbasi et al. 2008). These findings are consistent with my own research for this book as well. Not only are Furries more likely to not be heterosexual but they are also 'significantly more likely than members of other fandoms to identify as transgender' (Plante et al. 2016, 11). Many Furries reported the fandom as being a safe space for those with non-heteronormative sexualities and gender identities. The phrases 'accepting community' and 'self-acceptance' are seen across the data collected for this book; this may be an important part as to why many people who do not have a heteronormative sexuality feel so comfortable within the Furry Fandom.

The IARP research has been used extensively in my book because, quite simply, there is limited research on Furries from other scholars (though this minority does appear in my analysis when possible). I should mention that there are research conclusions from the IARP that I do agree with, such as fursona use and demographics, and there are parts of their research that I challenge. Up until now, the research on Furries has mostly viewed them as a homogenous group with members sharing these characteristics consistently. However, my book calls the conclusions of this research into question by identifying at least two different categories of 'Furry'. First, I have identified the 'lifestylers' who see being Furry as an integral part of their identity and who believe that they are spiritually or psychologically linked to an animal which has become their fursona. Second, I have identified 'hobbyists' – these are Furries who see their 'being Furry' as membership of a fandom and something that they see more as a pastime as opposed to being something that is a 'part of them'. In this book, I demonstrate the ways that these two distinct parts of the fandom interact and sometimes stigmatize each other. I illustrate how, despite being part of the same overall group, they construct their identity differently, making their fandom fractured at times while simultaneously still considered a fandom rather than splinter groups.

Methodology

Two common questions asked of scholars are 'why do this research?' and 'what is this piece contributing to the field?' With other studies on fan cultures, the researcher is often a fan themselves, which is their reason for creating their project. The principal rationale for this project was my general ignorance of the Furry Fandom and a desire to study a fandom that has so far been largely undocumented, aside from IARP research. It is interesting that despite an increasing participation of Furries in public spaces (such as conventions) in recent years in North America, the Furry Fandom is still largely unknown to many people and yet they have frequently been a punching bag for media institutions.

I think it is also important for me to address the fact that recent research from Ruth Deller has noted that 'just because we *can* research something does not mean that we *should*' (2018, 126; emphasis in original). Deller argues that ethical research must also consider beneficence to the fan community that is being studied, and this was something I especially had to think about when considering pornography. I will establish throughout this book the ways that Furries are stigmatized, and one of these is due to being named as 'sexual deviants' – and of course if I put research out into the world on Furry pornography I may draw unwanted attention to an already stigmatized fandom. However, Deller gives breathing room for looking at the context of the situation, and if the research can be presented fairly, this book would constitute that fairness as I use a non-judgemental gaze and because my conclusions may help destigmatize their group.

Data for this book was collected using survey program Qualtrics, which was distributed online, and ran for one month between October and November 2015. In that month, 1,020 individual responses were recorded from self-identified Furries. The Qualtrics questionnaire comprised questions which recorded both quantitative and qualitative data. This mix of ethnographic methods followed the principles of netnography as set down by Robert Kozinets (2010). I chose netnography as it is specifically designed for the monitoring of online communities as opposed to physical ones. Although, Furries do sometimes meet in the geophysical space, I have found that Furry communities proliferate predominantly online. The principles of netnography focuses on the content produced by members of the community which is why it was well-suited for the Furry Fandom. The process has five steps.

Step One: Definition of research questions, social sites or topic to investigate

The majority of Furry studies that have been conducted thus far have endorsed a preferential use of quantitative methods, mainly the use of online or offline surveys. This may be because they have been conducted by those in the field of psychology rather than the humanities. I wanted to find rich data to analyse as well, so I combined the two methods.

First, it was important to me to correctly identify the demographic population. This was crucial because there was a possibility that demographic data found in my study could have been different from the demographics found in the IARP studies. This was because many of the studies by the IARP collected their data at conventions in the United States. This meant that the majority of data was from Americans and also those who had the financial means to attend conventions. For Johnny Saldana, 'patterns demonstrate habits, salience, and importance in people's daily lives' (2016, 6), so by using demographic data it can be possible to see patterns emerge in certain age groups that is useful for the study. Ultimately, I found that much of my demographic data was similar to that of the IARP which gives a good indication that we have identified common demographic data.

However, I was concerned that much of the IARP research seemed to focus mainly on highly identified Furries, that is, those who saw being a Furry as an integral part of their identity. But for me, as a fan studies scholar, I am aware from my studies of other fandoms that not every fan is the same. Nor do they have the same identification levels with their fandoms as others. Therefore, my most important research question/topic was to investigate whether there was a pronounced difference in identification levels and how this affected fan practices in the fandom. In my research, I did in fact find that there is a very pronounced difference between highly identified Furries and those who considered themselves 'just fans', and I discuss these differences throughout this book.

Step Two: Community identification and selection

To make sure that a large breadth of Furries had access to the questionnaire it was hosted on Reddit in the r/furry subreddit messenger board. Reddit was founded in 2005 by Alexis Ohanian and Steve Huffman and has become one of the most popular websites today, with more than 330 million active users a month, organized by nearly 150,000 active communities, and 14 billion views per month. Reddit is a significant source of data for researchers due to the breadth of comments from users, with the highest number of comments on one discussion thread reaching 84,000.[6] Adrienne Massanari notes how Reddit is a rich methodological site describing it as 'a unique, boundary-spanning platform that elicits new questions about the nature of participatory culture and community in the age of social networking' (2015a, 7). Although it presents an opportunity for researchers, Reddit has not been without controversy. Researchers have noted that parts of the site have become a hub for misogyny, and media outlets too have called out specific subreddits such as r/theredpill and r/MGTOW (Men Going Their Own Way) as examples of toxic web communities (Baym 2015; Massanari 2015b). Despite the controversies described above, Reddit was still an appropriate forum to conduct my research. Reddit became a strong candidate as a research setting because an aim of my book was to investigate Furries who considered their engagement on a hobby level and to see how prevalent these members were. By using Reddit (where users often use the whole website rather than focus only on one subreddit) it was more likely that data would be collected from less identified Furries.

Another consideration for conducting the research was to address an issue which concerned how to access members of the Furry Fandom to invite them to partake in the research questionnaires. Due to the negative media portrayals that Furries have encountered there has been resistance to reporters and researchers approaching these groups. In *Furries from A–Z*, Gerbasi et al. (2008) asked the head of the convention they were researching to publicly support their research team. This was so that the attendees would know they were legitimately there to research and would not make fun of participants. When studying vulnerable or stigmatized groups, the underlying principle of the research must take consideration of the participants' well-being (Pyer and Campbell 2012, 312).

Furries in other studies have been pathologized as mentally ill people just playing dress up (Bryant and Forsyth 2012, 532). Even the sympathetic study *Furries from A–Z* tentatively created the term 'species identity disorder' (Gerbasi et al. 2008, 206) which could be seen as pathologization. The data was collected with the aim of providing an 'initial overview of the area of online communities' that the Furry Fandom inhabits. Kozinets does warn of the disadvantages of using questionnaires for exploring 'a new culture or community topic about which little previously was known' (2010, 43–5). This problem was overcome by using the demographics recorded in *Furries from A–Z* to create a starting point from which to base the survey questions.

Step Three: Community participant-observation (engagement, immersion) and data collection (ensure ethical procedures)

An approach that is sometimes used within the fan studies discipline is that of the scholar-fan approach as suggested by Matt Hills in *Fan Cultures* (2002) whereby the academic researching the fandom is also a member themselves. An important methodological distinction to note is that I am not a member of the Furry Fandom and was therefore researching the fandom as an 'outsider'. There are both pros and cons to this methodological approach. Henry Jenkins made the argument that he already knew many of the fan behaviours of the tele-fantasy fandom as he was an 'insider' (1992, 83). Hills built on this notion by referring to the scholar fan as a 'map maker' (2002, 18). By already knowing and being involved in their own fandom, these academics find it easier to connect various aspects together, forming the map of fandom behaviour.

Mapping any fandom often has to use dense description to put fan behaviour in context that becomes meaningful to an outsider of the fandom (lay person).

Due to the demographics of academia, especially pre-millennial-born, there has been criticism as to which fandoms have been deemed worthy of study. Mark Duffett levied this accusation in that it is often 'privileged middle-class commentators talk[ing] about their film, record and comic book collections or fan communities' (2013, 263). As a researcher investigating a fandom of which I am not a member and which has no connection to my outside research interests, was important as it actively invokes Guattarian and Foucauldian principles about power (which I will talk about in Chapter 2 and in the summary of this chapter). The issue that comes from being a fan of what you are studying is summarized succinctly by Jenkins; that he had a 'high degree of responsibility and accountability to the groups being discussed' (1992, 7). The power relations involved in being close to the study means that some data can be overlooked in preference to more 'wholesome' or gratifying data. Hills notes that academics can sometimes create 'moral dualisms' where academics drawing an 'us/them' distinction can create 'good' and 'bad' fans (2002, 20). The term 'bad' here does not mean that these fans behave badly as such, just that they may perform fan practices differently from other members of the same fandom. This is what Hills argues concerning the 'imagined subjectivity' of academics in that researchers can view different fan behaviour within the same fandom as 'bad' (2002, 5). This has caused issues in research as it 'can be used to restrict and pathologize specific cultural groups, while promoting the achieved 'normality' and 'legitimate' authority of others' (ibid.).

Researchers becoming overtly involved is not an uncommon approach in social studies disciplines with the popularity of ethnographies since the end of the twentieth century. Alan Bryman notes that 'postmodern ethnographies' have become increasingly popular, where the academic becomes overtly involved and 'often within the data and findings themselves' (2012, 463). However, there have been criticisms of this approach in recent years in other academic fields that being 'too close' to what you are studying can produce researcher bias, and fan studies have seemingly not been immune to this. In early fan studies scholarship, researchers often focused on the positives of fandom. In fact, Camille Bacon-Smith's work in 1992 did not even contemplate the possibility of fan hierarchies that are commonly researched today. Bacon-Smith even viewed fandom as an 'equalizer'. However, I do not have a direct connection with the Furry Fandom as a fan. Therefore, I feel that this gave me good academic and emotional distance from the research participants to be impartial with findings but not so far as to 'Other' the participants. I found that this also helped me when it came to data analysis as well.

Step Four: Data analysis and iterative interpretation of findings

My research used the idea that the more a key phrase or idea appeared in collected data the more likely it is to contain some significance (Marshall and Rossman 2011, 212). This would improve the consistency of coding with content analysis utilized as the framework for this. Conceptual coding was used as an analytical process as it focuses only on what is present in the data rather than preconceived concepts. After first coding the data to examine themes and develop theories, axial coding was used to help reflect the 'commonalities among the codes' (Marshall and Rossman 2011, 215). Due to the other studies in this area from the IARP, I predicted that most commonalities would show a negative experience with general culture for the Furries and their social lives. To make sure that interpretations of codes were within a reasonable level of accuracy and trying to cause minimal theoretical bias, peer debriefing to check codes was implemented. This was because peer debriefing is useful as 'different values regarding interest, time frame, and the use of findings' can differ between researchers (Cooper et al. 1997, 4).

As Kozinets and Garcia et al. (2009) predicted, netnographic methodologies have become increasingly popular, especially in research on fans; in the edited collection by Paul Booth on media fandom and fan studies, there were mixed method research conducted on several different types of fandom (Booth 2018). Martin Barker and Ernest Mathijs argue that mixed research methods can bring about clear ways of presenting and analysing complex data in fan studies (2008, 153). For instance, the difference between adverbial modifiers such as 'satisfactory' and 'Wow!' are treated as equal in quantitative data even though they show various levels of enjoyment (ibid., 152). Barker and Mathijs suggest that due to this, mixed methods can be more precise when fans are talking about their experiences. I thought this to be particularly important for the Furries because their experiences have not been well documented besides IARP research and only a smattering of other research papers; this is compared to the vast amount of research that has been done on the *Star Trek, Star Wars, Doctor Who, Harry Potter* fandoms and the like.

As well as this qualitative data, quantitative data collection was used to ascertain the demographic data of the participants. Although, as Barker and Mathijs suggest, numbers can never claim to be fully representative, Bryman states that it can provide a good base on which generalizations can be formed by researchers (2012, 635). Rich data from qualitative data collection can then be used in triangulation. For example, not only do I suggest that many Furries feel stigmatized due to their rating it on a numerical scale but my qualitative data also suggest *why* they felt stigmatized. This means that more conclusions can be drawn from the data which cannot be inferred by using just either method in seclusion.

When it came to analysing Furry pornography, I choose to analyse the images, themselves taking them at random from under the Not Safe for Work (NSFW) tag on FurAffinity. Furaffinity.com was an appropriate choice as there were plenty of submissions which fit the selection criteria. Coding through analytic memos was used because, as noted by Saldana, 'coding and analytic memo writing are concurrent qualitative data activities' and can help a researcher by triggering 'deeper and complex meanings' than when restrained by the parameters of a field note (2016, 44). This was chosen as it is compatible with coding and interpreting visual data:

> Repeated viewings and analytic memo writing about visual data documented in field notes or maintained in a repository are more appropriate approaches to qualitative inquiry because they permit detailed yet selective attention to the elements, nuances, and complexities of visual imagery, and a broader interpretation of the composition totality of the work. (Ibid., 60)

Step Five: Write, present and report research findings and/or theoretical and/or policy implications

Perhaps step five of Kozinets's netnography is seemingly obvious when one considers the fact that I have written this book. However, my research also led me to some policy implications when it came to studying online communities.

I found that there was a lack of consensus on what ethical protocols should be used when studying stigmatized fan communities online, so I decided to formulate them myself. This led to a peer-reviewed article being published in 2017 and I have been using it as a guideline for research into Furries under the age of 18 (Austin 2017a). The paper addressed the ethical challenges of researching an online community where there is a potential for harm in the real world. The article produced a step-by-step guide on actions to take if an online participant was threatening to harm themselves due to abuse such as reporting behaviour to the host website, reporting behaviour to a local authority if possible and revealing researcher status when doing covert research in times of crisis. However, I feel it is now important to focus on this book and what I have discovered in my research findings.

Summary

In 2013, a friend 'came out' as a Furry to me and was desperately worried that the friendship would end. They explained that they believed that the bad media attention the fandom had received would mean that I would wrongly label them as a sexual deviant. In fact, I had not heard of the fandom at all. The friend then introduced me to other Furries at a Furry gathering known as a 'furmeet' later that day and I found them to be nothing more, nothing less, than normal people (well in so far as anyone can be normal I suppose!). This led me to wonder why this group had been so badly stigmatized by the media, and thus led me to research and investigate, starting off with a pilot study when I was studying at the University of East Anglia, then a larger study when I was studying at Anglia Ruskin University and then finally this book.

This book addresses identity construction within the Furry Fandom that has been neglected in previous research. I use Gilles Deleuze and Félix Guattari and other post-human theorists throughout because highly identified Furries are examples of post-human embodying becoming-animal. I have, however, also situated my work in the tradition of fan studies as well because, although the Furries are often seen as different from fans, the Furry Fandom shares many traditional functions of other fandoms. For example, they have a thriving gift and commissioning economy just like other fandoms and adhere to a geek hierarchy (Busse 2013). In addition to this, there are Furries who we would not consider as highly identified or post-human because they simply see 'being a Furry' as a hobby. This has led to me extensively investigating this opposition within the fandom, highlighting the differences that occur depending on whether a Furry views their involvement as a lifestyle or as a hobby. I highlight the importance of viewing Furries who are hobbyists through a fan studies lens rather than a post-human one. When it comes to this identity construction, which is the backbone of my thoughts regarding highly identified Furries, I often use theorists who resist binary oppositions. This is important because I emphasize how the Furry Fandom presents as a postmodern fandom due to its heavy use of the online space.

Throughout this book I employ various parts of current research from the IARP, the most prevalent researchers in the area. The IARP use a psychological framework that was resisted in my work as it often homogenizes the Furries into one group. As I have already stated, I will demonstrate that Furries are a split fandom due to differing levels of identification. However, without their research, I would never have been able to start mine. I am profoundly grateful for the work they continue to put into their research which I believe has benefited the Furry Fandom immensely in trying to destigmatize them.

My aim is to build on IARP work from a different academic perspective as I believe this will provide long-term benefits to not only the Furry Fandom but also other fandoms which go on to delve into identity construction in an online context. Work by the IARP has been conducted on the way that Furries use concealment strategies because they feel stigmatized. My research has built on this to address the fact that Furries also suffered from in-group stigmatization. Although the IARP had identified popular species within the fandom, I believed it was useful to delve into this further and have used this book to explain the importance of fursona choice and how it relates to post-human theory for highly identified Furries.

Supported by research from the IARP, I note how often Furries are stigmatized for being sexually deviant. However, there had been little acknowledgement about pornography as a practice within the Furry Fandom academically at the time of my writing.[7] It was important to test the stereotype that Furry pornography promoted bestiality, as this may prevent Furries being stigmatized by these stereotypes in the future. I feel that this helps support IARP research aims in destigmatizing the Furry Fandom especially as it is difficult to declare something as not sexually deviant if we do not have facts and statistics to back up this claim. In this book I demonstrate my claims that pornography consumed in the Furry Fandom is for the most part the same as consumption of regular pornography. This is because I evidence the most popular motifs in Furry pornography, which are comparable with human pornography.

One of the issues that the Furry Fandom has had is that many people do not know what a Furry is, and some of those few who have heard about them have only heard negative stereotypes. From a fan studies perspective, it has become important to investigate these stereotypes due to the pathologization and stigmatization that has occurred unjustly in other fandoms. The data collected by IARP research was invaluable in providing a baseline upon which to collect demographical data for this research. I also 'map' the fandom to give the reader a robust list of Furry signifiers. This is because although the IARP have collected demographic data of the Furry Fandom, they have only partly identified Furry signifiers as Furries when it comes to inhabiting the online space and the implications of this. Pierre Bourdieu's work is used to situate this debate as his work has been used in fan studies (which is also used as a framework when describing Furries as fans) so was deemed appropriate. The concept of the habitus situates how the Furry Fandom online community establishes and enforces Furry signifiers and 'acceptable' fan practice. There are other instances where the Furries have been mentioned as working as other fandoms do in the online setting, specifically in Kristina Busse's geek hierarchy (2013). It was also important to address the fact that more recent online research suggests that many people now present themselves on the internet as 'themselves' rather than creating a false persona. Thus, I discuss how highly identified Furries use the online space and their fursona to enact their Furry identity which they cannot achieve offline (becoming-animal) and how Furries who use the fursona as a hobby enact their fan identity in a different way.

I have found what I believe to be an important correlation between the age that Furries began using Furry websites and when they 'became' Furry. This goes against some IARP research which has suggested that a Furry identity is a natural one, or is not chosen, rather than being influenced by popular culture. Which I argue against throughout this book when it comes to Furries who consider themselves as fans. The concept of the geek hierarchy (Busse 2013) which has been used extensively in fan studies is used to explain this behaviour. Furries tell other Furries what does and does not make them a Furry, and thus how to be a 'better Furry'. The online space is an important one for this fandom as they do not have a set media text. I evidence that because they do not have a set media text, the internet is the only place in which Furries can engage with artwork or other Furries the majority of the time; this can be due to the fact that many do not wish to be Furries in the real world as they are worried about stigmatization or because some Furries are not geographically close to any others.

I use Kristina Busse's geek hierarchy to explore the notion that fandoms (including the Furry Fandom) essentially work as institutions rather than simply communities. This is because fandoms fulfil two functions: distribution and measurement. Using Deleuze and Guattari, I argue that Furries distribute fan work (sometimes for profit) and that fandom participants are 'measured' for how good a fan they are. How fans perform their 'measuring' is done via the geek hierarchy within each fandom.

I investigate instances where there are issues within the fandom itself. One of these issues is the acceptability of viewing and use of pornography, especially that of cub fur, with its acceptability in dispute in the fandom. In IARP, research acceptance was often used solely as positive, whereas the data for this book has exposed that some Furries believe that the fandom can be *too* inclusive and *too* accepting. The examples I give reveal that there are internal fandom disputes as to whether being a Furry can also be a sexuality. It also shows that there is displeasure at other Furries' behaviours such as criminal acts – at Furry conventions by others and a perceived hierarchy of popular fandom members who are allowed to get away with such behaviour. This leads me onto investigating the intra-fandom stigmatization between highly identified Furries and those who saw being a Furry as a hobby; one of the main complaints from less-identified Furries was that they felt highly identified Furries were taking the fandom too seriously which has not been evidenced in any great depth thus far.

To build on the IARP work, I use 'event + context' to explain that it is not just the fact that Furries can be bullied online or offline, but the fact that it is deemed acceptable by media examples. The notion of 'event + context' means that it can be easier to situate marginalized communities with trauma that has affected their identity construction. By identifying the context for why the Furries feel they are stigmatized, it is easier to see how it developed within the community. I was interested to see whether Furries felt more stigmatized online or offline and whether those who saw Furry as an integral identity felt more stigmatized than those who were 'fans'. I found that there are differing levels of stigmatization depending on whether Furries were highly identified 'lifestylers' or less identified 'hobbyists'.

For highly identified Furries, stigmatization comes from the fact that they are currently enacting the modes as identified by Deleuze and Guattari of the 'Body without Organs' (shortened to BwO herein) – specifically those of the masochist body and the schizo body. Deleuze and Guattari (although they do not mention stigmatization by name) have noted that those who have 'undesirable' traits are often persecuted by the institutional system. Many critics of the Furries often judge the Furries as having a mental illness, and Deleuze and Guattari noted that those who enacted becoming-animal or BwO would be deemed as such. I believe that, in keeping with IARP work on biological essentialism and the Furry Fandom, those who see the Furry Fandom as a hobby feel far less stigmatized than those who are a highly identified.

Although the IARP's research had highlighted that canines are particularly common as fursonas and primates were incredibly rare, I investigate further fursona demographics. Like IARP data, I found that canines were extremely popular. After analysing comments and popular Furry texts I have come to argue that the concept of myth is appropriate in which to analyse why species were chosen. This was because many of the Furry signifiers attributed to fursonas were found in common Western myths concerning animals. Additionally, practicalities and artwork were also discussed in Chapter 4 as this is not something I had come across in IARP research. For Furries who see the Furry Fandom as their hobby, especially those who like to make or wear fursuits, species choice is influenced by practicality and economy. Furries who want to 'wear' their fursona must pick a species which can 'walk' on two legs because otherwise it would be impractical. Popular Furry artwork has also influenced which species are chosen and there has certainly been a preference across the fandom for 'cute' or 'Disneyfied' characters.

Although the concept of myth worked well for Furries identifying across the spectrum, it was important to note that highly identified Furries were also identifying with their fursonas on an abstract level. Theories by Deleuze and Guattari are used to show how highly identified Furries chose their fursonas in a way which personified 'becoming-animal'. To compliment Deleuze and Guattari, Donna Haraway is also included with her notion of companion species as an exploration of the historical link between animals considered as 'pets' rather than those used in agriculture, meat industry, science labs and the like. Companion species theory helps explain how the historical relationship between canines/felines and humans has influenced species choice within the Furry Fandom. This is why companion species are popular choices within the fandom because these are the animals that are most commonly available in positive representations in myth, popular culture and as pets.

The research for this book addresses the gap in literature on Furry pornography and presents conclusions and trends on which further study can be based. I evidence how Furry pornography has a certain aesthetic style similar to that found in anime and in cartoons and how Furry pornography is not representative of the real, physical animal. By using theorists such as Patricia MacCormack (and others), post-human pornography does not need to provide a realistic representation, and upon textual analysis of the images, these pictures are more credible as representing human desires. This has the interesting implication that the Furry pornography is not immune to human cultural and social standards when it comes to *what is hot and what is not!*

What some members of the Furry Fandom have done in their production and consumption of Furry pornography, however, is replacing the human body as the site of desire. When it comes to the concept of 'passing' online, many people often take the role of a gender/sexuality. which they are not able to enact in real life, for assorted reasons. There is a proportion of Furries who state that their fursona is a different gender and/or sexuality from themselves and thus use their fursona as a conduit in which to 'pass' in the online Furry world. Although lifestyler Furries are using pornography as post-human, that does not mean they have got rid of hierarchies, and in fact, whether they are a lifestyler or a hobbyist, they are reproducing a species hierarchy. Canines and felines are regularly used as fursonas and also appear most commonly in the pornographic images randomly selected for analysis for this book. And the most common animal traits such as pretty fur coats, doe eyes and nice pointy ears are being projected onto pornographic and even some non-pornographic fursonas to make them 'sexier'. I mostly focus on how Furries anthropomorphize their pornography through the use of human breasts and genitalia.

In conclusion, this book maps the Furry Fandom and its fan hierarchy from the fan studies discipline. This book brings together fan studies and theories of the post-human to analyse data gathered from members of the Furry Fandom. In this, I offer an overview of a previously less studied fandom, which offers insight into online behaviour, post-human identity construction and fan-produced online pornography.

2

Furries as fans

One can find furry meetups and fandoms around the world. Conventions give a space for people to learn new things, meet new friends, build up a business and more ... 'It truly is a loving community that wants to give back and show what it is really about.'

– Nelson (2019)

Fandom over individual identity

In my introduction to this book, I briefly noted that I would be approaching the Furry Fandom using two separate disciplines: post-human philosophy and fan studies. This may seem like a strange combination as usually scholars use overarching fan studies theories when researching a fandom. However, in the research for this book I found using one academic framework impossible because I have found that although there is 'a Furry Fandom', Furries are split into two different groups when it comes to identification and engagement and thus experience the Furry Fandom differently. It could be suggested at this point, why then, do I still consider two different groups to be the same fandom? Surely, they are a splinter group or should be considered different fandoms?

I argue that these two groups constitute a whole fandom rather than splinter groups because they inhabit the same fandom space and share many of the same fan practices and sometimes fan policing. Although they do not have a set media text like many fandoms, Furries create their own content and media on 'what it is to be a Furry'. Catherine Driscoll encompasses different kinds of fans in her definition: 'Fandom is a web of communities distinguished by type, pairing, and/or genre, with varied degrees of overlapping or interlocking membership' (2006, 93). This is the example I have used for the Furries as despite not having a set text, they have a strong community (mainly online) where norms and values are adhered to. Their fandom is created not via knowledge from an outside source then but by sharing their fan knowledge and creating fan hierarchies as identified in other studies (see Busse 2013 and Proctor 2013).

When it comes to fan practices, the Furries carry out many activities that are commonly seen in fandoms. One of these popular practices is fan-made erotica known in some fandoms as 'slash fiction', a common theme of Kirk and Spock love stories in the *Star Trek* fandom (Lamb and Veith 2014).[1] Jenkins was one of the first to write academically on the concept of slash fiction in his 1992 book *Textual Poachers*. He noted that 'the process of sexual fantasy is consciously explored in a large number of slash stories' (1992, 205). Similar scenes in books and online fiction from other fandoms were not as heavily regulated at this point in time compared to Furry conventions (Gold 2015, 29). Shipping practices are where fans place two established characters from a media text in a non-canon romantic relationship in their fan fiction and so the fan is external to the story. But slash fiction also offers a chance for an 'original character' to be included. For the Furries, they can use their fursona as the participant character. In other fandoms where a writer places themselves in a fan story, it is a practice known as Mary Sue.[2] Here the fan story becomes a stage for expressing more than their daily selves.

As discovered in the study of Gerbasi et al. (2008), there is a wide-ranging plethora of differing sexualities in the fandom, and it has been suggested by Furries that this is because it is socially acceptable to have discussions about sex and sexuality freely. Member of the Furry Fandom, Thurston Howl, notes that 'it is a sexually open fandom, and that openness plays into their art as well as their literature' (Howl 2015, 51). But due to this, the Furry Fandom has enforced very strict labelling practices in their Furry erotica from many of the early conventions in the 1990s. As conventions grew and younger members began to attend, Furry stories with one mildly explicit sex scene would be labelled erotica and not sold to younger members.

The Furries are also similar to other fandoms in the way that they 'measure' who is a fan and who is not. There is ample evidence to suggest that fans often separate what they deem as 'good' fans and 'bad' fans by measuring how *much* of a fan others are. Judgement is seen not just within individual fandoms but fandom as a whole. Hierarchization between fandoms has been especially noted by Busse when discussing how *Twilight* fans were treated at Comic Con in 2011;[3] 'the fannish object itself was dismissible, and the fans' new fan status and their modes of engagement were suspect' (Busse 2013, 73).

This is in line with the way Guattari theorizes an institution: 'It produces signifiers, not signification; it produces the institution and institutionalization, not a party of a line; it modifies the general direction of history' (2015, 219). This is especially relevant for fandoms. The signification for the fandom (the media object) is outside of the fandom and it is fans within the fandom who create their institution by deciding what signifiers are 'important'. Using Deleuze and Guattari then, it is difference between signifiers and the way fans distribute and measure other fans in their fandom. Fans not only do this with fans in their group but also when measuring their differences to other fandoms, and this has been particularly true for the Furry Fandom. For Deleuze this was to be expected as 'difference is monstrous. We should not be surprised that difference should appear accursed, that it should be error, sin or the figure of evil for which there must be expiation' (2014, 38). This can also be true for new fans trying to get further involved within fandoms. Being a new fan can bring difficulties as the new fan may not know the 'correct way' that fandom expects them to be a fan:

> When a subject wants to assert itself on the group level, it must first recognize that there is no place for it in the current state of social mechanics. It is then forced to intrude on, to cause violence to the existing system. (Guattari 2015, 64)

Consequently, much like in identity construction in general, a fan's new identity 'is discursively established through classifications: It includes and asserts a certain "horizon" of possible social positions as "positive" and it excludes others as "negative"' (Chouliaraki 2013, 304). One of the ways this is significantly done is the way a fan's behaviour is ratified 'by what the individual sees in the mirror of other peoples' reactions' (McCracken 2008). Judgement is one of the most important parts of identity construction in a fandom institution, in the perspective of Michel Foucault's theory on training and discipline. For Deleuze, 'judgement has precisely two essential functions, and only two: distribution, which it ensures by the *partition* of concepts; and hierarchization, which it ensures by the *measuring* of subjects' (2014, 43; emphasis in original) and fandom – and the Furries certainly fulfils these two essential functions.

Distribution of popular fan creations can have a strong and sometimes dire effect on the institution of fandom; partition of concepts has even caused violent reactions within the fandom. In October 2015, a user on Tumblr named Zamii070 was bullied into attempting to commit suicide by members of the *Steven Universe* (Sugar 2013–19) online community due to their consensus that her fan artwork was not 'acceptable'. The reason for why her work was unacceptable was not that it was bad fan art (not technically proficient) but because she had drawn the characters 'wrong'; her main 'transgression' being drawing the character of Rose Quartz thinner than she was portrayed in the cartoon, which to some fans made her fat-phobic (Austin 2017a). The abuse that came flooding onto her Tumblr profile sent a clear indication to other fans that her distribution of 'unacceptable' fan art was wrong as it did not adhere to fandom signifiers. Zamii070 should have followed the partition of concepts as set out by the institution and had been be roundly punished. It can be argued that it is unsurprising that many fans who looked up to *Steven Universe* for having diversity in characters to have this reaction: 'Our construction and presentation of a public persona draws heavily upon the definitional resources that movies [in this case a cartoon] make available' (McCracken 2008, 119). For fans who felt better represented by having larger set cartoon characters Zamii070's interpretations was seen as deviant and not true to the source material. This partition of concepts is seen in the Furry Fandom as well, with Furries' behaviour towards others who draw 'unacceptable' fursonas and this is known as 'policing'.

The process of alienation within fandom has been discussed extensively in fan studies when discussing how fan hierarchies occur and how behaviours of fans are 'policed'. For Scott, the motivation of fans to police their boundaries is a well-intentioned one, 'about protecting, rather than controlling, the ideological diversity of fannish responses to the text' (2009). For others, policing has been to actively silence the 'wrong' interpretations of their chosen text.[4] Cornell

Sandvoss in particular argued that every fandom has a 'policed set of beliefs' (2011, 60), and Stanfill endeavoured to demonstrate that to exist as a fan required two elements to be understood by the fan themselves. Stanfill noted that fans had to be '(a) immersed in dominant ideas about the "right way" to interact with the media and (b) emotionally invested in a subculture that is often understood to violate those norms' (2013a, 118). I agree with Stanfill over other fan studies academics who can sometimes have a more sympathetic view of fans policing themselves. For example, Booth and Kelly gave an optimistic view when discussing *Doctor Who* fans. They describe fandom as 'offer[ing] a voice to the traditionally voiceless, autonomy to those typically lectured-to' (2013, 60). But, that fan voice is only allowed to be articulated if it is within the norms of that particular fandom, those who are deemed as either too involved or not involved enough are often pushed aside as manifesting the 'incorrect way' to be a fan (Busse 2013, 84).

Another commonality that the Furries share with other fandoms is negative stereotyping of fans. A prevailing stereotype in most fandoms is the gender of participants as mostly male, with the fan often shown to be a nerdy beta male, unsuccessful with women, a nervous attitude and a spotty complexion (Scott 2011; Geraghty 2014). Science fiction fandoms are a good comparison for the Furry Fandom as they share this negative stereotype as perpetuated by the media (to be discussed in depth in Chapter 5). Fans being 'nerdy' and beta males is a prevailing stereotype with mainstream media happy to portray sci-fi fans as this, seen in, for example, *Big Bang Theory* (CBS 2007–19), *The I.T Crowd* (Channel 4 2006–13) and *Chuck* (NBC 2007–12). Even shows which feature women as the 'nerds' like *30 Rock* (NBC 2006–13) still show the 'nerd' as socially awkward, not conventionally attractive and obsessed with 'nerdy things'. In the Furry Fandom this is taken a step further, with Furries being portrayed in mainstream media as beta males with 'deviant desires'. A tendency for people outside fandoms to incorrectly pathologize or fetishize members of certain fandoms has appeared not just in the Furry Fandom. Female fans are often accused of fetishizing or sexually desiring their chosen media object. Duffett notes that in the 1940s, female fans were evaluated as being under 'swoonatra'-ism as opposed to being women who could enjoy the music of Frank Sinatra without a romantic component (2013, 8).

The Furry Fandom has often been presumed to be a sexual fetish fandom, television episodes like the *CSI: Crime Scene Investigation* (CBS 2000–15) episode 'Fur and Loathing in Las Vegas' (05/04) broadcast unsympathetic storylines portraying Furry conventions as no more than sex orgies (Plante et al. 2014, 2). This kind of portrayal was seen again on *The Entourage* (HBO 2004–11) episode 'The Day Fuckers' (04/07) which focused on perceived deviant sexual behaviour of the Furries. The study of Gerbasi et al. therefore noted that there was in fact an 'empirical void' when it came to whether these assumptions concerning Furries were correct (2008, 199).

It is important to bring a more balanced and wider view of identification in the Furry Fandom as there is still evidence that wider society often pathologizes fans who they deem as too identified with a fan object. Among the media, Channel 4, in particular, has been conspicuous in pathologizing fans using titles such as *Crazy about One Direction* (Channel 4 2013), which literally labelled the fans included in the documentary as crazy and overzealous in their participation in the One Direction Fandom. Channel 4 also had a documentary series entitled *World of Weird* (Channel 4 2016) and the second episode of the series focused on the Furries. Once again, the inclusion of the word 'weird' in the title portrays Furries as 'not normal'. These misconceptions have made their way into academic works with researchers associating Furries with plushophilia:

> Some persons with plushophilia – and some persons who apparently do not experience this paraphilia – at times wear anthropomorphic animal costumes called *fursuits* (Gurley, 2001). The practice of wearing fursuits to impersonate animal characters is called fursuiting: an erotic interest in doing so could appropriately be called *fursuitism*. (Lawrence 2009, 206; emphasis in original)

This section in Anne Lawrence's work is problematic for two reasons. First, the way it is phrased could suggest Lawrence is unconvinced that not all fursuiters have plushophilia. This suggests that she is pathologizing all Furries as suffering from a sexual 'disorder'. Second, Lawrence's reference to the activity of fursuiting comes from an article in *Vanity Fair* by George Gurley (2001) entitled 'Pleasures of the Fur'. The article as a reference is problematic as many Furries complained that the piece portrayed the fandom not only inaccurately but also unfairly, and pushed the narrative that it was solely a sexual fetish fandom. This idea that the Furry Fandom has a sexual fetish for plushophilia and having sex in fursuits has been shown as inconsistent in the data collected by the IARP. Although many definitions of Furries in the mass media includes 'wears a fursuit' (Winterman 2009), studies have found that the vast majority of Furries do not own them, largely due to the huge costs in making one (Gerbasi et al. 2008, 205; Plante et al. 2014).

Stereotyping of Furries as sexually deviant has persevered in media as evidenced by the television shows referenced here already. This book challenges these misconceptions not by ignoring the sexual part of the fandom (because as with all fandoms there is one) but by addressing it; the only way to dispel inaccuracies are to research and analyse them. It is common practice for fan studies researchers to study their own fandom and there is sometimes an unwillingness to draw attention to the darker side of their own fandom. Duffett states that 'all stereotypes contain a grain of truth, but it is the generalization and misinterpretation of that kernel that creates the problem' (2013, 40), which is why I made clear in my methodology that I wanted to avoid this.

Other fandoms commonly covered in research have a set media text on which fans create their identity. Although this may seem to preclude the Furries from calling themselves a 'fandom', I give a defence as to why they should still be considered under this title. A *Star Wars* fan can be identified because they state that they like an aspect of the media surrounding the *Star Wars* franchise – they may have enjoyed one of the movies or read a good fan fiction or anything in between (Proctor 2013). Furries, however, create their own content and media, which means that 'what it is to be a Furry' stems from multiple sources. There will be some who would still count themselves as Furry but may not go on the same sites or create fan art leaving some of the Furry communities disjointed from one another. Therefore, Furries count as a fandom (even without a base text) because they exhibit a fandom community where norms and values that create a Furry identity occur. This moves away from studies which have specified a source text around which a 'community' is based. A more important part of fandom then, is the interaction between fans and their peers. Janice Radway argued for engaging in subversive reading of genres where readers were assumed to be passive in *Reading the Romance* (1984) and I employ this thinking in my research.

Catherine M. Ridings and David Gefen (2004) suggest that virtual communities have three defining features: shared interests and goals, a sense of permanence and frequency of interaction. In fan studies, the concept of a virtual community becomes even more complicated due to the tendency of virtual fandom communities to end when the media text is no longer relevant, that is, when a TV show gets cancelled, notably called post-object. These communities cease to fulfil the three defining features suggested by Ridings and Gefen because after the TV show ends, community members no longer visited; they no longer needed to have discussions over the direction of the storyline, possible romantic attachments and the like because there would never be any new material on which to speculate or bond over. Rather than their fandom being based on a fan object or media text, the Furry Fandom ends up being related more so to community or individual engagement. This means that Furries (and other fandoms not based on a media text) have far more ontological security than those that do. This is because there is little disruption of self-narration or identity construction as it is not based on a media that could be cancelled or changed by outside influences. Lawrence Grossberg noted that the abundance of popular culture in late modernity has given ground for fans to 'construct relatively stable moments of identity' (Grossberg 1992, 59). Therefore, interaction with their chosen media texts means they have been able to 'organize their emotional and narrative lives and identity' (ibid.). Therefore, this can have consequences when disrupted – when Disney was announced as the new owners of the *Star Wars* franchise, pessimistic fans vocalized their concerns on Twitter. For some *Star Wars* fans, Disney did not coincide with their preconceived vision of how the franchise should be run, or indeed the direction the fandom should take. They were concerned that their beloved franchise would be subject to 'Disneyfication' (Proctor 2013, 204).

Furries will never have this problem, their fandom cannot be changed by an external factor such as a television show being cancelled halfway through or a book series ending. This also means that the Furries can often avoid comparisons between fans about who is a 'better' Furry because there is no 'external' fan knowledge on which to judge. This is indicative of the

Furry Fandom being a postmodern fandom rather than a more traditionally structured one (around a media text). Although definitions of 'postmodern' can vary and is often used to describe types of art, Marita Sturken and Lisa Cartwright argue that

> postmodernity refers not just to a style and a form of subjectivity that emerged in late modernity. It also refers to changes in the social and economic conditions that help to produce these styles and ways of being a subject. (2009, 313)

Within fan studies and indeed this book, postmodern is referred to in terms of the way that fandoms are not stagnant institutions and thus there is not one 'truth' and way to being a fan:

> The postmodern is distinguished by the idea that there is not one but many truths and that the notions of truth are culturally and historically relative constructions. (Sturken and Cartwright, 2019)

Postmodern societies grant more fluid options to 'truth' when it comes to identity especially in online space as the online space gives a person an opportunity to act out an identity they may not be able to in real life (Gauntlett 2008, 105). In the postmodern world, sexual identities (not acts) are socially constructed and some Furries feel their identity is outside the norm (Haenfler 2010, 74). This could indicate why a notable proportion of them do not identify with heteronormativity, compulsory or otherwise. Judith Butler's influential book *Gender Trouble* written in 1990 famously set about to explain this shift into self-reflexive identity narratives where gender was now no longer set but performed every day. This was building on Erving Goffman's notion when he declared in *The Presentation of Self in Everyday Life* (1959) that identity was often a 'performance'. Anthony Giddens went on to expand on this stating that 'a person's identity is not to be found in behaviour ... in the reaction to others, but in the capacity to keep a particular narrative going' (1991, 54). David Gauntlett supported this theory in that not only was identity a performance but that nothing within identity was fixed (including gender). Gauntlett stated that identity was 'little more than a pile of social and cultural things which you have previously expressed, or which have been said about you' (2008, 147). With the increased reflexivity that is found in late modernity, it not only 'enables the development of a self-narrative' in a fandom

(Williams 2015, 20) but also facilitates increased access to the sociological and cultural conditions on which this self-narrative can occur. Therefore, through interaction with their chosen media texts they have been able to 'organize their emotional and narrative lives and identity' (ibid.).

Furries, in particular, are seen as a lower order of fandom compared to the now more mainstream fandoms. In the works by Busse (2013) and Francesca Coppa (2014) they both acknowledge that the Furry Fandom is often deemed as the lowest rung on the 'Geek Hierarchy'. Although there is no specific event which has led to why Furries are viewed as a lower order of fandom, the IARP have pointed to the way that there are stereotypes of Furries that have been disseminated by the mass media. This may have influenced the view of the Furries from other fandoms and created stigma. Judgement in fandom can change at given points however:

> Difference … in no way represents a universal concept (that is to say, an idea) encompassing all the singularities and turnings of difference, but rather refers to a particular moment in which difference is merely reconciled with the concept in general. (Deleuze 2014, 41)

This sentiment is echoed by Guattari:

> Identification with the prevailing images of the group is by no means static, for the badge of membership often has links with narcissistic and death instincts that it is hard to define. (Guattari 2015, 227)

This issue has occurred in post-object fandom, situations where the fandom's media text (such as a television show) has ended. Judgement changes when media texts come to an end and identity construction as a fan of an ended media text can also end. For Rebecca Williams, 'media texts are crucial to the development of reflexive self-narratives' (2015, 22) and when there is no longer a text to build on the narrative stops. For *Resident Evil* franchise fans, cultural referents are important when going from the video games to the film adaptations; they recognize that these texts are in the same universe because there are points in the game which have the same characters from the movie, for example (Lay 2007). When these cultural referents are not adhered to (such as in the new *Star Wars* movies with a supposedly canonically inaccurate Black Stormtrooper), some fans were less sure about their fan identity because the canon had been suddenly interrupted, getting rid of some of their cultural referents (Proctor 2017). As noted by Booth, the more dispersed a media text is, the more able a fan is to create a salient identity in which to insert themselves within the fandom (Booth 2010, 162). For Furries, not having a set text means that they are more easily able to construct their identities, but that is not to say that Furries can do whatever they want and still be called Furries and be part of the Furry Fandom. As with other fan communities, there is still a social hierarchy and a 'map' to follow (Hills 2002, 46).

When discussing television fandoms, Jenkins made a distinction between 'zappers' and 'casuals' (Booth 2010, 19). 'Zappers' would flick through different shows compared to 'casuals who enjoy specific shows but do not make specific effort to watch them live on air' (Booth 2010, 19). Jenkins would not class either of these people as 'true' fans, and it becomes much harder to do this when dealing with a non-television or media-based fandom such as the Furries. Although Jenkins's definitions of 'zappers' specifically refer to television watching, the basic principles of casual engagement can be applied in a wider fan studies context. For the Furry Fandom, for instance, should we consider those who invest money in purchasing a fursuit as 'better' fans than those who do not? There is of course a problem with this question, because fursuits are incredibly expensive when well made, so why should we specify that rich Furries who have the means to buy these get to be the better fans? My answer to this is that there are no 'casual' Furries, there are only Furries who express their Furry identity in different ways. I have split the Furries into those who see it as a hobby and those who see it as a post-human identity but resist all calls to state that one is more 'invested' or 'truer'. They are just different sides of the same fandom which need to be approached differently when it comes to analysis.

Fan identity construction

So far in this book I have noted the way that membership of a fandom constitutes an identity, agreeing very much with the IARP that it is a process of 'authenticity'. However, discussions on what is 'authentic' when it comes to the Furries has often been presumed rather than investigated in as much as with ideology, it can be so pervasive that social interactions come as 'common sense'. Althusser uses the example of hailing a person in the street:

> Assuming that the theoretical scene I have imagined takes place in the street, the hailed individual will turn around. By this mere one-hundred-and-eighty-degree physical conversion, he becomes a subject. (1971, 48)

Althusser suggests that the reason that the individual who turns around to respond to the hail only does so because they have been conditioned to do so by ideology. He proposes that these behaviours are taught by the ideology and so become the social norms of the society (rather than common sense):

> What thus seems to take place outside ideology (to be precise, in the street), in reality takes place in ideology. What really takes place in ideology seems therefore to take place outside it. That is why those who are in ideology believe themselves by definition outside ideology. (1971, 49)

When studying fandoms, Althusser can be useful in this sense because thus far in research many assumptions on Furries have been made on 'common sense'. It has been taken as 'common sense' that they have fursonas and fursuits without looking into the reasons why they do this. Because it is just assumed that these are identifiers of someone within the Furry Fandom, there has been a lack of research into 'hailing' behaviour.

Bourdieu's theory on the habitus is indicative of the problems of the assumptions of hailing. In that a fandom is a kind of habitus where fans use their social standing to create hierarchies, and these are not just 'common sense' but ideological as well. The word habitus is used to describe the outside environment in which we find ourselves in due to our life experiences. Habitus refers to the way in which different norms are reproduced depending on the conditions in which the person finds themselves, that is, which society at what time period:

> The *habitus* ... provides practices which tend to reproduce the regularities immanent in the objective conditions of the production of their generative principle, while adjusting to the demands inscribed as objective potentialities in the situation, as defined by the cognitive and motivating structures making up the habitus. (Bourdieu 1977, 78; emphasis in original)

Bourdieu is particularly useful for this book as his theories have been used within fan studies before:

> His work on processes of cultural distinction offers a way for theorists to analyse how fan 'status' is built up. It allows us to consider any given fan culture not simply as a community but *also as a social hierarchy*, where fans share a common interest while also competing over fan knowledge, access to the object of fandom, and status. (Hills 2002, 46; emphasis in original)

As Althusser wrote that ideology and thus status is reinforced in society, Bourdieu (as noted by Hills 2002) showed that status could also be built up: 'every material inheritance is, strictly speaking, also a cultural inheritance' (1984, 77). Bourdieu's theory of cultural capital argued that as well as economic capital improving a person's societal class and social standing, increasing their economic wealth improved their cultural knowledge. In fan studies this theory has been applied to the way that fans construct their fan identity, how they become 'better fans' in the eyes of other fans. A good example that Bourdieu uses to illustrate the benefits of cultural capital is that of the school system. Bourdieu discusses the answers to a survey where participants of different social classes were asked to name classical composers. He found that there was a direct correlation between education level and number of composers answered, with those in clerical and managerial jobs faring the worst (Bourdieu 1984, 12–13). Bourdieu argues that children in a 'higher' social class are more likely to be taught about classical composers than other children and thus have more cultural capital. In the study of Gerbasi et al. (2008), this idea of cultural capital was applied (even though it was not a primary focus of the study). When testing 'typical' stereotypes of Furries, Gerbasi et al. (2008) noted that there was a consistency in stereotypes that 'Furries recall liking cartoons more as children than others', 'Furries like science fiction more than others' and 'Furries are employed in computer and science fields' (ibid., 204). The consistency found with these stereotypes suggests that Furries grow up in a habitus where it is common to watch cartoons and science fiction shows. Also, it can be suggested that Furries often live in a social class where access to technology is possible. In a collated edition of IARP research over five years it was found that 75 per cent of Furries have some post-secondary education (Plante et al. 2016, 12).

For Bourdieu, and for fans, activities are used to 'prove' a person's social and cultural capital to others:

> In the absence of the conditions of material possession, the pursuit of exclusiveness has to be content with developing a unique mode of appropriation. Liking the same things differently, liking different things, less obviously marked out for admiration-these are some of the strategies for outflanking, overtaking and displacing which, by maintaining a permanent revolution in tastes, enable the dominated, less wealthy fractions, whose appropriations must, in the main, be exclusively symbolic, to secure exclusive possessions at every moment. (1984, 282)

Within the Furry Fandom, the way that Furries perform their fandom to each other can 'prove' their Furry cultural capital within the fandom group setting. Good artists and well-known members (popufurs) in the Furry Fandom are an example of cultural capital gains within a fandom. The location where cultural capital really mattered when it comes to identity construction therefore happens in Bourdieu's habitus:

> The *habitus* ... provides practices which tend to reproduce the regularities immanent in the objective conditions of the production of their generative principle, while adjusting to the demands inscribed as objective potentialities in the situation, as defined by the cognitive and motivating structures making up the habitus. (Bourdieu 1977, 78; emphasis in original)

Bourdieu's theories, like Althusser's, mainly focus on identity construction on a macro level meaning that an identity is constructed by outside forces acting upon the body rather than an individual affecting their own identity construction. This is important as it echoes, and in part helps to explain, hierarchies that are found in Furry communities online, which I discuss later in this book. However, I also use Foucault to supplement Bourdieu and Althusser when it comes to Furry identity construction as their writings often see institutions and the habitus as repressive. For Foucault, 'if power were never anything but repressive, if it never did anything but to say no, do you really think one would be brought to obey it?' (1984a, 61). Ideology, therefore, is not used to punish (Foucault's previous point that there would be no point if ideology always said no) but to 'train' individuals in correct behaviour for a reward of conforming (1984b, 188). Within the Furry Fandom, this notion of how ideology works can be discussed in the way that some species are chosen over others. Although it appears that a Furry is not 'punished' for picking a species which is unpopular, the mechanisms of Furry ideology can make it less likely for a Furry to choose a less well-known species which may explain why certain species are oversubscribed (see Chapter 4 on species choice).

An important idea of Foucault that I have applied in my book is concerning the 'regime' of truth:

> 'Truth' is to be understood as a system of ordered processes for the production, regulation, distribution, circulation, and operation of statements. 'Truth' is linked in a circular relation with systems of power which produce and sustain it, and to effects of power which it induces and which extends it. (1984a, 74)

The regime of 'truth' creates ideologies and thus how one constructs their identity permeates through all interactions in society. This influences how certain identities are viewed as acceptable and how nonconforming ones should be punished. Furthermore, different institutions can interplay and create multiple ways of constructing identity. Media institutions have caused issues for the Furry Fandom as they have promoted the idea that being a Furry is 'deviant' by spreading unfavourable stereotypes in television programs. In the online context, this has meant that a regime of truth has been created that being a Furry is a nonconforming identity. This has led to some Furries experiencing stigmatization for their identity. Foucault and regimes of 'truth' as a concept has been used in fan studies with Proctor's work in relation to the representation of female fans: 'fans may actively partake in policing, but media reportage and representation also collaborate in the construction of a (gendered) regime of truth' (2016, 68). When discussing new documentaries on fans, Proctor noted that 'mainstreaming' opens up previously hidden ideologies for media outlets to mine as evidence of homogeneity and 'freakishness' (ibid). Foucault's 'regimes of truth' can help show how Furries are having to construct their identities in relation to the power aspects of media representations. This is certainly prudent in relation to accusations of Furries being mentally ill or sexually deviant.

Guattari's work was in agreement with Foucault's that institutions that create the signifiers for norms and values can be changed again and so regimes of truth could be malleable. But Guattari argued that signifiers changing is often for antipathetic or negative reasons rather than Foucault's hopeful ones: 'identification with the prevailing images of the group is by no means static, for the badge of membership often has links with narcissistic and death instincts that it is hard to define.' (2015, 227). This has been seen within the Furry Fandom in several instances including media representation when it comes to the 'acceptability' of pornography consumption. I discuss this in relation to the split within the Furry Fandom when it comes to pornography within the fandom themselves in that parts of the group want to distance themselves from it so as not be stigmatized as mentally ill or deviant.

Identity construction from a Guattarian standpoint then is that a person must understand themselves not just in opposition to 'the Other' such as in Foucault's work but in relation to all the multiplicities in their own body. Contrary to other theorists who say identity is constructed from how a person understands how being homosexual is different to heterosexual, Guattari builds on theories of 'becoming' he developed with Gilles Deleuze. To be a homosexual is not just within the realm of sexuality (since sexuality will also affect other parts of the person's identity) and so must be understood as a whole and not just by its binary pair. Deleuze also looked at identity in an abstract way, not just in binaries.

Building on Sigmund Freud's notion of the phallic stage in development, Deleuze theorizes the way in which this can be used to establish not just a sexual identity but also a linguistic identity and thereby a cultural identity. According to Freud, although men have a physical penis, no one can in fact possess the symbolic phallus. This is why Deleuze refers to it as an empty object, in that the symbolism of the phallus is not fixed and can change depending on events in the current society. Furries and Therians offer an opportunity to argue that identity is an empty object. Furries and Therians who identify heavily with animals and would consider themselves not as wholly human can hold this identity because its significations do not need to be 'true or false'; Scientifically or medically, a person cannot transform into an animal, but that does not mean their identity cannot incorporate it in symbolism.

Deleuze does not prescribe to the top-down theory where all cultural knowledge is filtered down a hierarchy but is in fact due to the interconnection of multiple singularities and so not only compliments Althusser and Bourdieu but also builds upon them. As well as this, it suggests that identity is more complex in that it can be actualized in random ways and is not just garnered from 'real' experience but also that which is experienced unconsciously, that is, the impossible and the possible.[5] This is relevant in discussions on how cultural trauma can occur with fandom groups and I discuss this specifically in the chapter of this book that discusses stigmatization.

Assigning animals important roles in interpretation across the centuries with animals appearing in dreams, symbolism and poetry across cultures has been pointed out by Deleuze and Guattari (Deleuze and Guattari 2013a, 275). And this is essentially what the Furry Fandom are doing in their use of the animal and how lifestylers, in particular, construct their identity. Deleuze and Guattari use three main archetypes when discussing the animal: Oedipal, state (also referred to as the Jungian archetype) and demonic. Oedipal animals are the animals which have become too anthropomorphized (specifically as a substitute child) in animal studies, in its 'tendency to remain too close to animal rights discourse with its liberal, Oedipal vision of the subject' (Bednarek 2017, 52). The Oedipal animal is to be resisted in theory as it often imposes a familial hierarchy on certain animal species (Gardner and MacCormack 2017, 3). Instead, using the Jungian and demonic archetype theories utilized by Deleuze and Guattari becomes a more appropriate way to resist this oedipal reading in animal studies. In their discussions on 'becomings' in a *Thousand Plateaus*, they are described as the 'process of mimesis [that] brings nature and culture together' (2013a, 275). The Jungian and demonic archetypes are important to consider with the highly identified Furries in the Furry Fandom as they suggest becoming rather than *imitation* of the literal animal – resisting the Oedipal structure and thus launching a becoming-animal.

These theorists were chosen because they exemplify the different ways we construct our identity. This has been increasingly important, because as I have noted, previous research has seen Furries as being highly identified. However, I have made a distinction in my work between those who see the fandom as a hobby and those who see it as integral to their identity. Otherwise, we risk 'falsely bounding' this community as Duffett has argued has happened with other fandom research.

Lifestylers versus hobbyists

My aim in this segment is to identify the ways in which identity construction happens for the Furries in two distinct ways and to determine whether a Furry is what I have termed either a 'lifestyler' or a 'hobbyist'. I have done this, because although as I have mentioned that different fandoms have different levels of engagement, it still forms a singular fandom without the debates that have plagued fan studies theorists of 'who is a better fan'.

In *Furries from A–Z*, a hierarchy was formulated from a Furry typology. In their typology, the IARP came up with four categories of Furries:

1. Undistorted and Attained – The Furry sees themselves as 100 per cent human and do not wish to be 0 per cent human.
2. Undistorted and Unattained – The Furry sees themselves as less than 100 per cent human but would not wish to be 0 per cent human.
3. Distorted and Attained – The Furry sees themselves as 100 per cent human but would become 0 per cent human if possible.
4. Distorted and Unattained – The Furry sees themselves as less than 100 per cent human and would become 0 per cent human if possible. (Gerbasi et al. 2008)

My issue with this typology is that it presumes that all Furries are highly identified with being a Furry. This is because it assumes that Furries will all see being 'Furry' as a part of their identity. Even the Undistorted and Attained category presumes that a Furry thinks about their identity within the fandom at a post-human level, even if they are not adhering to its principles at the current moment.

The main reason why I found myself making the distinction between two types of Furries is because this was the main trend out of all the data I collected – those stating they became a Furry as a result of indulging in fandom activities and media consumption, and those who 'always knew' that there was some part of them that is animal, which led them to finding the Furry Fandom. Furthermore, their seminal paper from 2008 gives me two distinct reasons why I also make this distinction. First, because their data shows that Furries experience affinity with the fandom in the way that can be studied under fan studies and, second, because they uncover evidence of some having a post-human affinity with being a Furry without realizing it.

In their paper, they focused on common stereotypes about Furries that have been pervasive on the internet, using these as a measure to find out how 'consistent' these were compared to Furries they researched. The first goal was to test the Furry stereotypes and to determine the 'common denominators' (Gerbasi et al. 2008, 199). Their secondary goal was to investigate the aspects of possible gender identity disorder, but instead of the feeling of being in the wrong body it was being the wrong species, tentatively named 'species identity disorder' (ibid., 200).

When it came to the results of their primary goal, it was found that many of the stereotypes applied to members of the Furry fandom were only somewhat consistent with the experiences of Furries (ibid., 204). Many of the stereotypes were typically those that were levied towards other fandoms – specifically, the nerdy 'fanboy' stereotype. Their secondary goal led to their declaration that there was a significant proportion of Furries who could be described as having 'species identity disorder'. They claimed that most Furries displayed the markers of those who would be classed as having 'gender identity disorder' (ibid., 214). Their largest group ($n = 77$) comprised Furries who would not describe themselves as less than 100 per cent human and would not wish to be 0 per cent human (later termed as 'undistorted attained type'). Their next biggest group ($n = 52$) considered themselves to be less than 100 per cent human and would become 0 per cent human, a type which comprised 25 per cent of the Furries from the study (ibid., 215). Of course, it is acknowledged at the end of the study that as at that time there were no other peer-reviewed papers to compare to, this created limitations on their conclusions (ibid., 220).

One of the main concerns that I had with the work of Gerbasi et al. was the use of phrase 'species identity disorder' for two major reasons. First, it denotes pathologization of a fan and, second, it uses a human versus animal binary. This is problematic when it comes to my classifications on Furries, either as fans or as post-humans. In a critique of the *Furries from A–Z* study, Fiona Probyn-Rapsey suggested that the use of the term 'species identity disorder' should be considered controversial due to its use of gender identity disorder theory as its basis. As well as this, there was little literature review on the topic before the term was introduced (2011, 294–5).[6] In a rebuttal to Probyn-Rapsey's comments, Gerbasi et al. responded as follows:

> We were not addressing the validity or political correctness of the gender identity disorder diagnosis (which is beyond the scope of *Society & Animals*). Given our word limit and the novelty of research on Furries, it would have been counterproductive to review the gender identity disorder literature. (Gerbasi et al. 2011, 303)

The above response gives their reasons for the inclusion of the term, but I would suggest that the term is still problematic. To label any fan as having a disorder of any kind is reminiscent of the descriptions of fans 'as fanatics'. As well as this, Gerbasi et al. specifically mention gender identity disorder in their abstract as having parallels with their new disorder construction. In light of this, there should have been at least some explanation as to what gender identity disorder is for the reader to understand the new term. This is especially important as Probyn-Rapsey points out that it is 'a highly controversial diagnosis that has been criticized for pathologizing homosexuality and transgendered people' (2011, 294). I therefore disagree that a review of the term by Gerbasi et al. would have been counterproductive. The use of gender identity disorder to categorize Furries into solid categories is at odds with work on fan hierarchies (Busse 2013). Studies on how *much* of a fan people are show that often fan identification with their fandom can be much more fluid; fans do not always share the same affinity for their fandom object all the time (Hills 2002; Proctor 2013):

> Our cautious suggestion of species identity disorder in some members of the Furry Fandom was based on our finding that many Furries agreed with statements that paralleled sentiments of people with gender identity disorder regarding their biological sex (e.g., 'A feeling that you are your non-human species trapped in a human body'). (Gerbasi et al. 2011, 302–3)

This is where I began to realize that there was a post-human aspect of the Furry Fandom that could not be fully realized in the psychological framework used by the IARP or by fan studies. This is because the above quotation suggests that the study was speciesist in that Gerbasi et al. are putting the notion of the human above the non-human animal.[7] This is something that I argue against when it comes to post-human theory, and for many people, 'what it is to be human' can have different connotations. Consequently, regarding anyone who does not identify as 100 per cent human as suffering from species identity disorder is challenging. This just raises more questions than it answers as Gerbasi et al. did not clarify what they meant by 'human'. The inclusion of highly identified Furries by IARP suggests that it is a common occurrence, with 46 per cent participants in their study supposedly having some form of species identity disorder. Also, by using the term 'less than 100 per cent human', it is homogenizing all other species into the group of 'non-human' and so relates back to a dominant human versus nonhuman model which this book challenges. Their study suggests that the most identified members of the fandom will 'definitely' have species identity disorder, but I have found this not to be the case in my research; in as much as my evidence demonstrates, there are Furries who greatly enjoy and are heavily involved in the fandom but would not wish to be less than 100 per cent human. And, conversely, there are Furries who do not go to conventions or get heavily involved in Furry activities but who would consider themselves less than 100 per cent human. This is contradictory to the idea of who this so-called disorder affects in terms of the study by Gerbasi et al.

Within this book, the title of 'species identity disorder' is not be used as it is not conducive to the tone or style of this research. This is because I find the typology categories too constricting and that is why I have instead used the broader categories of hobby or lifestyle; as with every other fandom, there are those whose life is all about being Furry compared to those who dip into the fandom every once in a while, and everything in between.

Although I have noted that identity construction can happen in the same way for both types of Furry above, it needs to be distinguished when it comes to analysing the way that lifestylers versus hobbyists engage in certain parts of the fandom; later in this book I will fully explore the ways in which lifestylers and hobbyists use their fursona in different ways, experience different levels of stigmatization and have differing engagement and views on pornography.

However, I have outlined here for reference how I began to separate the two parts of the Furry Fandom using IARP research.

When it comes to the fursona, previous research by the IARP has produced evidence that Furries use their fursona in different ways, and I have identified this in terms of fan behaviour (hobbyist) and lifestyler behaviour. Part of the IARP (Reysen et al. 2015a) investigated a Furries connection to their fursona and any perceived benefits to this and whether there was a relationship between chosen fursonas and in-group projection and in-group bias. Using social identity theory as a base, they noted that in a person's social group there is a hierarchy of favouritism behaviour. Talking about soccer fans, they responded that they are 'more likely to help fans of the same team than fans of a rival team in an emergency situation' (ibid., 49). There have been suggestions by other academics that in-group bias is due to self-enhancement or collective action. The study by Reysen et al. focuses on 'in-group projection' as being a possible cause (ibid., 50). In-group projection relates to fan hierarchies when it comes to fans who are not members of a fandom that society views as 'acceptable'. Reysen et al. categorizes these members as 'not-prototypical' and 'experience greater prejudice than members of more prototypical fan groups' (ibid., 50). Their hypothesis was that Furries would strongly identify with both the subgroup (Furry Fandom) and superordinate group (varied species within the fandom). They also found that there was in-group favouritism; its 'presence can be explained, at least in part, by in-group projection' (ibid., 55). They found that a Furry will be particularly biased in favouring their own fursona species and this can be related to fan hierarchies, prominent examples of this are found in research conducted in the *Doctor Who* and *Star Trek* fandoms; it has been found that fans will like their favourite incarnation of The Doctor above other actors' portrayals of the character, or a particular *Star Trek* series or Captain. This research showed that there are strong indications of fandom behaviour which could be studied under fan studies theory.

It was a shame that this study limited itself to just ten popular species and the fact that they did not include information from the Furry community. This data is easily available regarding the fact that sometimes fursona species choice is related to sexual stereotypes as well, commonly to choose a fox to show that you are hypersexual and submissive or a wolf to show you are wanting to be sexually dominant (Howl 2015, 52). When considering the work by IARP it is understandable why they chose to omit this information as they would not want their study to be read as a fetishization.

Although this research focused on the 'fan behaviour' aspect, I found that it created scope for investigating post-humanism because of its process of how different Furries identify with their fursona which could be investigated using post-human theory. To gauge how participants identified with their fursona species, they were asked to rate how strongly they agreed with three statements (adapted from their previous research):

1. I am emotionally connected to my fursona species
2. I strongly identify with my fursona species
3. My fursona species is part of me. (Reysen et al. 2015a, 52)

In their results, they found that identification with one's fursona and identification with the Furry community were 'significantly above the midpoint of the scale' (ibid., 53). This led to the IARP also stating that Furries relationship with the animals that they anthropomorphize and is related to their 'subjective wellbeing' (Roberts et al. 2015a, 534). Three main research foci of the research were to what extent Furries had an

(1) admiration or reverence for animals,
(2) spiritual connection with animals, and
(3) identifying as an animal. (Roberts et al. 2015a, 534)

Roberts et al's first hypothesis was that the more a person identified with a certain animal or animals would be how much they would want to anthropomorphize them. They wanted to prove that this person would ascribe positive secondary emotions to the animal as well (ibid.). They also hypothesized that Furries who identify as less than 100 per cent human would view themselves as an animal species as opposed to human and that their psychological well-being would then be 'related to the nature of their connection to animals' (ibid.). Their results seemed to affirm their hypothesis to the extent that Furries did tend to ascribe human traits and emotions to their fursona in a positive way as they liked or felt spiritually connected to the chosen animal (ibid., 540). They found that those who felt a spiritual connection to animals '[were] significantly positively associated with both life satisfaction and self-esteem' (ibid.).

A concern I had with this work is that their literature review exclaimed that 'much of the [previous] research has treated the human–animal connection as one-dimensional' (ibid., 534). This is astonishing considering that the question of the animal and its relationship to human beings has been debated rigorously in animal studies and post-humanism. Current literature is far from one-dimensional especially as writings by Haraway, (2003, 2008), Matthew Calarco (2008) and MacCormack (2009, 2014, 2020) all discuss how our relationship with non-human animals is changing to (hopefully) a non-speciesist and non-hierarchical one. In fact, much post-human theory is concerned with demolishing the human versus animal hierarchy. Had they been more aware of post-human theory, they may have realized that those Furries who were experiencing a personal spiritual connection with the animal can be considered as post-human.

As I have noted, I use theory from Deleuze and Guattari when it comes to signification and how it can create an identity. For Deleuze, signification matters because in post-human theory we do not hold it in a binary – that is, what is true compared to what is false. In terms of identity, this means that signification can have different meanings for different people and thus a different construction. Therefore, those Furries who gain signification from the animal and incorporate into their identity (despite it being physically impossible) have a human–animal connection which is post-human. However, this proves my point that when it comes to fursonas, one of the most important 'signifiers' of being a Furry, there is a clear delineation between those who see it as a fan object and those who incorporate it into their identity and are thus more identified with being a Furry itself.

Conclusion

When it comes to Furries who see being Furry as an integral part of their identity, we should be seeing this as a post-human lifestyle rather than being deviant or pathological. But this also gives us clear issues with trying to use a fan studies discipline in which to study them, which is why I have used the approaches mentioned above throughout this book. The Furry Fandom is a community of people who 'enjoy' the same thing, but they do so in different ways and in various states of identification and so it is important that research reflect this.

I have used theorists in my work who do not subscribe to using binaristic oppositions in theory and when describing human behaviour and this may seem at odds with my declaration of lifestylers versus hobbyists. However, I want it to be clear that I do see the Furry Fandom as a spectrum rather than in opposition. The easiest way to reflect this is the variances between a staunch fan-only identity and a post-human Furry identity. And this is what the rest of this book will now reflect upon.

3

The Furry habitus

Even in the socially awkward realm of the nerd fandom, you do need to interact with others to really make it a fandom in the first place. From the greymuzzles to the tabletop gamers to the boozy furs, the furry fandom has a huge variety to choose from.

– Shoji (2015)

Online location of the Furry habitus

Howard Rheingold is an academic who became one of the early users of the internet and documented his journey along with other academics' analysis in several books including *The Virtual Community*. For Rheingold, the internet was a utopian instrument in its creation, and humanity 'invented ways of using computers to amplify human thinking and communication' (1994, 66). Rheingold noted that 'the definition of "acceptable use" has expanded as the result of pressure by people who wanted access' (ibid., 84). And indeed, it cannot be denied that many technological advances were made by ordinary people who just wanted to make their lives easier:

> Global Usenet was created by a couple of students in North Carolina who decided it was possible for computer communities to communicate with each other without the benefit of an expensive internet connection; hobbyists in Chicago triggered the worldwide BBS movement because they wanted to transfer files from one PC to another without driving across town. (Ibid., 67)

Early academic research on the internet may seem irrelevant in terms of how the internet is used today; however, there are some key concepts which are still theoretically relevant to this book and this research. As seen in the offline space, using the internet to disseminate information in a helpful manner to other users was noted as building knowledge and social capital: 'I can increase your knowledge capital and my social capital at the same time by telling you something that you need to know' (ibid., 60). This concept of building social capital online has only changed slightly in as much as the technology has allowed it to grow. In Rheingold's WELL forum he could increase his social capital by sending good information, this has grown in virtual communities with people being able to visually show their social capital – in *World of Warcraft*, gamers can show their excellence at the game by using virtual possessions that have high value on their avatars, thus increasing their social capital (Pinto et al. 2015, 399). Whether rightly or wrongly, depending on who you ask, social capital can also be expressed online on social networking sites by using visuals to indicate how much social capital you have: '"it is not what you know, but who you know that matters", except that network sociality also views the *numbers* of people known as similarly important' (Willson 2006, 80; emphasis in original). This suggests that the online space follows the same principles set out by Bourdieu's habitus.[1] Social and cultural capital can ultimately affect a person's standing even though they are not sharing the same space.

Geographical space has been an important aspect in traditional identity construction theories such as Bourdieu's theory of the habitus; a person is influenced by those around them in their geographical space, such as primary socialization in the family and secondary socialization in institutions. For Karl Marx and Georg Wilhelm Friedrich Hegel, close geographical space meant that people could form their identity in binary opposition. For Hegel, this was the way in which the 'master related himself to the servant mediately through independent existence' (2003, 13). A master could distinguish himself as independent in this society because he was not chained as his servant was and it was in this way he could figure out his social existence in the world. Marx also theorized on binary oppositions:

> Even when he proclaims himself an atheist through the intermediary of the state, that is, when he declares the state to be an atheist, he is still engrossed in religion, because he only recognizes himself as an atheist in a roundabout way, through an intermediary. (2003, 20)

Even when the geographical space is extended to the national level, for Marx and Hegel, a person still constructs their identity via this geographical space and in oppositions. For Furries, however, encounters in a physical space can be problematic. This can be due to not having any Furries in close proximity to them, but also due to fear of stigmatization and physical harm. The fear of physical harm in particular may in part be blamed on the chlorine gas attack on the Mid-West Fur convention where nineteen people were injured and required medical attention. Not only did many Furries feel frightened of attending conventions after this attack but many felt even more stigmatized by the media and wider society as it was not taken seriously at all.[2] Additionally, the culprit was never found. In both my research and that conducted by the IARP, many Furries reported they feel safer having their Furry identity solely online as they are liberated from the normative gaze. This is due to their perception that offline society stigmatizes them and thus many do not want to enact their Furry identity in a geographical space. In my research, I found that only 9 per cent of respondents were happy to openly be Furry around strangers in public.[3]

The mainstreaming of fan identities has meant better knowledge of fan practices in general society so that some fans are no longer seen as 'odd' (Booth and Kelly 2013, 69). However, many Furries feel that this has not happened for them and so are still not welcome in a geographical space. Lev Vygotsky theorizes that identity formation occurs due to collaboration (1978), and for Furries in this study this is certainly not found in the geographical space as many did not know any Furries in real life.

One of the significant changes that is visible from early academic work today is that, not completely unsurprisingly, early academics did not envision 'the Net' being used regularly by non-academic persons. Rheingold theorized that the internet would not come into people's lives at the young age it does now: 'in the future, that's where the net culture in the rest of society will come from worldwide – those who connected with it in college' (1994, 68). But Rheingold was right to acknowledge that 'you can't just pick up a phone and ask to be connected to someone who wants to talk about Islamic art or Californian wine' (1993, 23). This is why the online space rather than the geographical space is more important for Furry identity construction. If many Furries do not choose to express their Furry identity offline, then there is nowhere for them to collaborate to create an identity *apart* from the online space. There are Furry conventions, which have become quite popular over the past ten years with increasing attendance, but these are not the places where a Furry finds out about Furry identity. A Furry going to a convention already knows what a Furry is and what being part of the Furry Fandom entails. A convention or fur-meet only reinforces the Furry identity that the person has already come across in the online space.

Furry signifiers in the habitus

Unlike most other fandoms or even identity construction in general, there is no geographical space to which they can go to find out 'how to be a furry' making the online setting the primary site where Furries' norms and values are socialized and coded as Furry. So, what signifiers can we find in the Furry habitus?

Signifier: Age and 'Becoming' a Furry

Age is an important demographic to consider when conceptualizing an identity construction. Victoria Carrington noted that in early education research, children were considered as 'unworldly' and 'experiences of childhood, including interactions with textual landscapes, are predicted and limited' (2005, 21). Before the internet, children traditionally learnt from school or the family. For Carrington, new media has led to the creation of the 'worldly' child who 'creates and distributes information and who has the capacity to independently access expanding sources of information' (ibid., 22). This change in how children are viewed when it comes to knowledge and practices is not surprising because, as with adult identities, children's identities are context specific and dependent on the society they are living in (Marsh 2005, 29). Growing up in a multimedia world is certain to affect a child's identity. Mean-making for a child cannot be seen in isolation or just simply from the traditional primary sources of socialization (ibid., 36).

For Herbert Mead, the time where a child begins to construct their identity is when they have unstructured downtime; a child understands and utilizes their own responses to stimuli while they are playing (2003, 34). A child 'responds in a fairly intelligent fashion to the immediate stimuli that come to him, but they are not organized. He does not organize his life as we would like to have him do, namely, as a whole' (ibid., 35). Mead recognizes that a child is inherently different from theories of identity construction concerning adults. This is because they have not had enough information (namely, life experience) to be able to construct a coherent identity so, instead, they play and therefore play with identity. While playing, a child is also able to evaluate the reactions of those around them, figuring out which attitudes are acceptable and which are not (ibid., 37). In this sense, children understand a fundamental aspect about identity in that 'staying the same person then means, in this case: remaining the same even when conditions, and even one's orientations, have, precisely, not remained the same' (Straub 2002, 65); a child adapts to the condition around them and the way that people react to them continuously.

Yet some scholars put identity formation as occurring in earnest in puberty; Erik H. Erikson (1968) suggests that identity formation usually occurs between the age of 12 and 20. As per my data, this is the age when Furries often 'discover' or start creating their Furry identity. In addition, this age often correlates with first visitations of Furry websites. Although there are some Furries who allude to knowing that they were a Furry before they had heard the term, most Furries in my study are the opposite in that they consume Furry media and then become part of the fandom.

My hypothesis then became that Furry identity is something that is learned for most people rather than being an inherent identity; it is specifically influenced, as other fans in other fandoms are created, by coming into contact with the media content and then developing a fannish identity from there.[4] This conclusion would be in keeping with the research by Reysen et al. who felt that their own results 'highlight the normality of the furry fandom, in so far as Furries are motivated by the same psychological needs as members of any other group' (2016, 614). However, this goes against other IARP research that views it as an identity you are born into, and the presentation in their research that being a Furry is likened to 'coming out'.

Signifier: Types of artwork

In studies on other fans, it has been found that they use the internet to influence media texts related to their fandom (Booth 2010, 158). This is found in the Furry Fandom because when it comes to the dissemination of artwork (like fursonas), this builds a Furry culture of what is acceptable and also what is deemed as 'good'. The internet is important for this in that without it there would be little access to Furry art by Furry artists in geographical space. In addition, there would be no cultural reference point for most Furries who have a solitary identity to 'judge' this artwork in relation to the Furry identity as this is often found by interactions with others. Other studies by the IARP have shown that content creation (like Furry art) is very popular (Gerbasi et al. 2008, 198).

Throughout my research, Furry artwork was mentioned extensively as one of the regular activities that 'made' someone a Furry. Since there is no set media text for the Furry Fandom on which to base their fandom, the Furries have created their own consumption culture when it comes to commissioning artwork. They have decided among themselves to establish norms for Furry art rather than being influenced by advertising and branding. That is not to say that Furry artwork has not been influenced by the mass media as many pieces hold a similar style to anime or the styles of Western animation. However, there is disagreement when it comes to boundary setting practices with regard to artwork in the Furry Fandom. There were concerns by Furries that some artwork was too sexualized or that people had failed to separate NSFW art and SFW art online.

Although Dick Hebdige (2003, 115) noted that the Disney brand was often viewed as innocuous, he suggested that it had more impact than originally believed. The IARP found that many Furries in their primary study 'recalled watching cartoons significantly more hours per week' than the average child, and this is significant (Gerbasi et al. 2008, 205). However, although these animals are anthropomorphized, they are not inherently Furry in nature. None of the Disney films consciously or subconsciously encourage children to create a Furry identity, although liking these kinds of films may inspire someone to like anthropomorphized images which then could lead them to find more online. Just because someone enjoys these images does not make them a Furry immediately. They would need to go on and engage with the community or other construction activities before we would give them this label.

Peter Wagner suggests that identity is predominantly related to meaning, and that these meanings not only guide identity construction but can also constrain it (2002, 5). The Furries have imposed their own meanings on the artwork they use for certain animal species, which is specific to Furries rather than to anthropomorphized animals in general. For instance, Furries often engage in role play when speaking to others online, that is, speaking as if they were the species of their fursona and as such different species have been given different coding (Shoji 2015, 14). This includes sexual stereotypes, such as having a fox fursona within the community signals to others that you are both submissive and hypersexual (Howl 2015, 52). These stereotypes are certainly not learned in the offline space of cartoon artwork or Disney imagery. The Disney Corporation especially try to keep their brand as 'family friendly' and so would certainly not be encouraging sexual stereotyping of their anthropomorphized characters (Hebdige 2003, 114). They are more than willing to sue those who use their copyrighted characters in a way that could affect this image (ibid., 116).

Instead, Furries are using intertextual knowledge gained from both cartoons and 'Disneyfied' artwork and the knowledge gained from the Furry Fandom. A study on young children and their knowledge of *Rugrats* demonstrated that they could make a connection between the TV series and the video game, even though they were not able to read (Carrington 2005, 18). They were able to identify visual similarities between the two to know that both were from the *Rugrats* franchise. For Furries, then, they are able to see an anthropomorphized character and identify whether it is 'just' a cartoon character or a fursona, that is, does the character have any of the Furry signifiers such as neon colours, wearing certain fashion, a unique name, is it a popular fursona species?

Signifier: Fursona and fursuits

In sociology, it has been common to say that subgroups form their identities in relation to the dominant culture (Stanfill 2013a, 121). What has not been discussed in any academic work thus far are the different subgroups that have occurred within the Furry virtual community. The hobbyist and lifestylers in the Furry community have different consumption practices especially when it comes to fursonas and fursuits.

Murat Oztok argues that knowledge construction online is often performed in virtual communities 'whereby participants share, utilize, cultivate, negotiate, and critique knowledge' (2016, 162). This is especially true in online fandoms where 'sharing continues to emerge as an integral part of fannish production' (Booth and Kelly 2013, 58). It not only establishes group norms but also increases knowledge around the chosen media text with conversations on canon, what makes good fan fiction, and other knowledge that is important to being a fan (Baym 2000).

One of the main issues that occur when academics try to describe online spaces as communities comes when looking at the research regarding who interacts within the community itself. Research has shown that most participants in online communities generally take three forms:

1. Answer People – These are the people who respond to postings from other members on a regular basis but rarely initiate conversation themselves.
2. Discussion People – People who both partake in conversation and initiate it.
3. Lurker – People who do not participate actively but frequently visit the community without announcing their presence (Baym 2015, 97).

This creates a problem since the most common group found in the vast majority of communities is that of the 'lurker'. In that respect, it becomes incredibly hard for an academic to gauge how much of an influence or importance the community has on that individual: how can it be assessed that someone is part of the community if they do not participate in any meaningful way? For the Furries, I use Heidrun Friese's theory in that 'if reality denotes becoming, then this becoming is not, as will be said later, the unity of being and not-being. For being is not a continuous self-identity unity' (2002, 20). An identity created online in a virtual community is not in an either/or relationship and the internet allows identities to occur that do not have to be in relation to anything else.

Less identified Furries who may not engage in online activities as much as highly identified Furries are still Furries despite different consumption habits. In online communities, lurkers are still enacting an identity, an identity which influences how they act online as a lurker. Although non-fursona holding Furries were less likely to go online daily (52.6 per cent) compared to those who had fursonas (70.9 per cent) or those who had two or more fursonas (77 per cent), they were still likely to go online regularly. Another 33.9 per cent of non-fursona Furries go online for Furry-related activities at least 2–3 times a week. When looking at Furries in general who go online 2–3 times or more a week, the results were very comparable: 91.8 per cent of Furries with fursonas were in this category, 93.5 per cent of Furries with two or more fursonas, and 86.5 per cent of non-fursona Furries also going online more than 2–3 times a week. Consequently, there is no huge variation with heavy online Furry activity between those with fursonas and those without.

'Individuals assume and enact identities based on available material and symbolic resources' (Oztok 2016, 160) such as movies between discussion and answer people. Following Friese's idea, the identity of lifestylers who believe they are part animal or would like to be part animal is still an identity even though it will never be realized. Michele A. Willson argues that 'loss of departure' (2006, 69) due to being able to access the internet seemingly at any time traditionally led scholars to understand online and offline identity bleeding together to make a coherent identity. Furries may consider they have a 'Furry' part of their identity even though they only interact with it online. This is a new kind of identity that doesn't need to be removed from the online context but still part of identity, just accessed at different times. Seminal psychoanalytic theory by Freud helps to explain this:

> We have two kinds of unconscious – the one which is latent but capable of becoming conscious, and the one which is repressed and which is not, in itself and without more ado, capable of becoming conscious. (2003, 30)

Although the IARP state that an almost universal part of being a Furry is the creation of a fursona, my study found that an astonishing 24 per cent of respondents of the 1,011 results did not have a fursona at all. This shows that having a fursona is still in the majority but it opens up questions as to why a significant minority do not have them but still consider themselves a Furry. The IARP research states that most Furries typically identify with a single fursona, and other research has shown that it is uncommon for a Furry to have more than two fursonas at one given time. This is mirrored to some extent in my own research. But, my work additionally reveals that a Furry is more likely to have no fursona over having two or more. In other studies, a fursona has been described as having two functions when it comes to identity construction: showing a social identity and a representation of a possible self (Roberts et al. 2015b, 45). In my research, I found that people who have multiple fursonas mostly use them as characters, rather than a representation of themselves. This was most common in the hobbyists and they had no real attachment to them and could change them on a whim, usually due to aesthetic reasons:

Furry: Was a bat first, couldn't figure out how to make the wings work in art
Furry: I have changed the colours of his fur to make him more aesthetically interesting as a character
Furry: I originally had a Wolf, but changed it when I learned about Fennec Foxes, and wanted to be *slightly* more original

For lifestylers, having multiple fursonas was rare and changing their fursona was usually based on a change in their personality or mental state:

Furry: My fursona is, for the most part, an idealized version of myself. Since the definition of my 'ideal self' shifts during significant changes in my life, my fursona must shift as well.
Furry: As I grew up, my fursona grew up with me, gaining more womanly features and becoming more colorful as I stepped out of depression

There was also another aspect to some lifestylers who use the fursona as a conduit because they feel trapped in a human body and used it as 'escapism'. And there were some clearly negative sentiments to those who were deemed 'too highly' identified with their fursona (distorted unattained type from the work of Gerbasi et al.).[5] However, there did seem to be a fluid social approach to the two groups in other comments from those who either use it as a representation or as a performance. Therefore, there is some flexibility in constructing the fursona identity without 'choosing sides' within the fandom, though as with other fandoms, lifestylers can be viewed as 'weird' by other members.

These results raise interesting questions about identity construction as it is contrary to the IARP research that previously thought the fursona as an integral part of Furry identity construction. The fursona is still common, but it raises the possibility that a Furry can be a Furry without a fursona or fursonas for a sustained period especially if they are still visiting the Furry online habitus on a regular basis. Once again this highlights a gap in academic literature due to the sole focus in research on highly identified Furries. Therefore, although fursonas are an important *indicator* that someone is affiliated with the Furry Fandom, this does not necessarily mean that a person is highly identified with their fursona. In fact, they may not see it as an integral part of their identity at all.

The IARP study by Reysen et al. (2015b) researched the difference in personality traits between a person's Furry fursona and their non-Furry identity. This is the only study by the IARP which considered that there could be a distinct difference between a Furries fursona and their non-Furry personality. Consequently, this research did not treat the Furry identity as something all-encompassing and integral. Their discussion centred on self-categorization theory: 'people are more likely to adopt these stereotype-consistent thoughts, feelings, and behaviours when they strongly identify with the group' (ibid., 92). From the social identity perspective, they used the 'Big Five' personality traits which are modelled around five factors: extroversion, agreeableness, conscientiousness, emotional stability and openness (ibid., 91). They claim little research has been done to show whether a person's prototypical traits from their 'main group' remains salient over time. Their research performed 'in the context of fans, looking at whether the salience of one's personal and fan identity will affect their self-reported personality scores' (ibid., 92). They started with a hypothesis that Furries' personality ratings would differ when it came to self-categorization. This was depending on whether they felt that being a Furry was part of their personal identity or whether they felt it was part of their fan identity. They found that many Furries rated their fursona identities more highly than their own personalities suggesting that 'fursonas represent idealised versions of the self that include, among other characteristics, outgoingness and confidence' (ibid., 94). The study then went on to compare their findings to sports fans and found that sports fans' rating of their 'sports fan identity' differed from their own personal identity 'except for openness to experience' (ibid., 96). This suggested to Reysen et al. that the 'difference in personality scores caused by identity salience was not unique to Furries and does occur in members of other fan groups' (ibid.). They concluded that personality is not stable throughout a lifetime as suggested by other studies.[6] Instead, they aligned with other studies that it depended on which identity is most important to the individual at that given time.[7]

For many Furries, their fursona is an important part of their identification in the Furry Fandom, and in this book (as with IARP research) a Furry will often use their fursona as an idealized version of themselves. The study of Reysen et al. found that 'all five personality traits were found to be stronger in Furries' Furry identity than in their non-furry identity' (ibid., 96). What is relevant for what I found in my research is that the study by Reysen et al. suggested that Furries who do have fursonas have a practical use for them and this was corroborated by my own findings. These fursonas are incorporated into their identity in the offline world rather than being art that is bought simply for pleasure. Even if a Furry is a hobbyist, they still have a practical use for the fursona by using it as an identifier that they are members of the fandom due to aesthetics, even if they do not identify with it in the same way that a lifestyler would.

In studies by the IARP, fursuits have been consistently popular with Furries. Fursuits are well liked even by those who do not own them. But as with other studies, they are less common than many outsiders would presume. Only 81 respondents out of 995 in my study owned full fursuits, but it should be noted that 60 per cent of the respondents said that they would like to own one.

As with other studies, the reason many gave for not owning one yet was often due to the huge cost of making a full suit (Plante et al. 2014, 15). For the best suits animatronics are often used, which are highly complicated for a layperson to make. But I also found that 32 per cent of respondents would *not* want to own a fursuit. This may be because of the different environments that these studies were conducted; *Furries from A–Z* and many other IARP studies were conducted at conventions. Participants may have bought their fursuits or

Furry articles of clothing for making their own full fursuit for the convention (as it was a special occasion) or even at the convention itself. Though my research shows that there are Furries who do not want to own a fursuit, it does suggest a trend towards ownership in the majority. I would state then that fursuiting is a common phenomenon within the fandom; whether it takes the form of watching others do it or owning a suit themselves. This is supported by similar findings by the IARP. Fursuiting is clearly a social characteristic within the Furry Fandom, and thus to want to aspire to owning these suits is a social norm which is why they are a common sight in the Furry habitus.

Signifier: Furry vernacular

Vernacular creativity in the Furry Fandom is mainly conveyed by the way they anthropomorphize animals. But what I want to make clear in this book is that not everything that is anthropomorphized will be related to and liked by the members of the Furry Fandom. Therefore, what anthropomorphization 'counts' as Furry has to be identified and this can be demonstrated by 'vernacular creativity' (as discussed by Jean Burgess (2006) and Ryan M. Milner (2012)). This vernacular creativity is symbolism that is understood by a particular community, and a good example of this is memes. A meme, for example, has to include shared symbolism for the meme to be considered appropriate by the other members (Baym 2015, 70).

Memes were described by Limor Shifman as follows:

a) *A group of digital items sharing common characteristics* of content, form, and/or stance;
b) That they were created *with awareness of each other*;
c) Were circulated, imitated, and transformed *via the internet by many users*. (2014, 6; emphasis in original)

For example, many popular movies have many memes that are shared and that include characters and quotes from which anyone who has seen the film (or knows the basic plotline) would probably recognize. However, in work on trolling, Whitney Phillips (2015) noted that often memes were used as 'lingua franca' and that often they had a deeper meaning that would baffle outsiders.

This is also seen in Furry communication and vernacular in that you have to be part of the fandom to understand the symbolism behind the artwork and certain commonly used words.

To demonstrate in general, a particularly popular meme from the cult movie *The Big Lebowski* directed by the Coen Brothers uses a sample from a scene where the character Walter angrily states 'am I the only one around here who gives a shit about the rules?'[8] On Reddit, 'Am I the only one around here,' and the picture of Walter to go with it, is used to convey a multitude of statements which have nothing to do with *The Big Lebowski* scene at all; the meme format is simply to air their grievances around an unpopular opinion including not listening to a popular artist, watching a popular sports event, not liking a popular food and so on. To someone who does not understand this meme they would then be confused as to why the film scene 'has been wrongly quoted'. With lurkers, then, we can assume that they will understand the references being made in their own community and thus show an 'example of shared practice that requires a sense of group identity' (Baym 2015, 87). Although they are not 'practicing' the memes as lurkers, they understand the meaning of the meme and would be able to replicate it if they chose to. These shared practices also affect the norms and member expectations of the communities. Fursonas, when used as avatars, can be considered to have vernacular creativity as they transmit membership of the fandom through symbology; the way the avatar is drawn uses aesthetics which are known to a Furry but may just look like a random animal drawing to outsiders. Unfortunately, many Furries in my study do not use vernacular creativity outside of Furry websites because trolls online also recognize their symbology and can attack them. This is because trolls are often not lay persons but individuals with specific knowledge of 'underground' online identities.

As shown with other subcultures that have been researched over the years, there is an established Furry vernacular which is used across the fandom. This use of slang is common in online spaces in fandoms as online spaces 'encourage less formal interactions' (Booth and Kelly 2013, 64). Although slang and vernacular has traditionally been associated with adolescents, it is common to see slang terms used in fandoms (Androutsopoulos and Georgeakopoulos 2003, 4). In fan studies, it has been discussed that having knowledge of the common vernacular of any group provides others with the knowledge of whether the person is an 'insider' or not (Van de Goor 2015, 276). This can be related to geek hierarchies as discussed by Busse that using appropriate vernacular shows 'how good of a fan' a person is and thus cements their position within the fandom. The role of vernacular has been important in queer subcultures as well such as isiNgqumo spoken by Black, Zulu men and Polari spoken by predominantly white British gay men.[9] These languages allow members of these communities to communicate without the fear of being outed as these sexualities were illegal at the time. For the Furries, vernacular is a useful tool to communicate with other Furries when they may not wish to be seen or associated with the fandom by a lay person.

Deleuze identifies three types of relations that occur within propositions in language. The first is that of denotation:

> Denotation remains external to the order which conditions it, and the true and the false remain indifferent to the principle which determines the possibility of the one, by allowing it only to subsist in its former relation to the other. (2004, 22)

Denotation is used as a frame of reference by language users and it determines how people interpret the language that is used to form an understanding, which will be influenced by their cultural knowledge. What is being said does not need to be 'true' but it needs to be 'known' by those receiving the information. Second comes manifestation when talking about a given object; there must be some sort of frame of reference so that the speaker knows what the object is, but their manifestation of the object does not have to have a regard as to whether it is 'true' or not in language. This is influenced by the final relation in proposition which is that of signification:

> The law governing two simultaneous series is that they are never equal. One represents the signifier, the other the signified. But thanks to our terminology, these two terms acquire a particular meaning. We call 'signifier' any sign which presents in itself an aspect of sense; we call 'signified' on the contrary, that which serves as the correlative to this aspect of sense, that is, that which is defined in a duality relative to this aspect. ... Thus, the signifier is primarily the event as the ideal logical attribute of a state of affairs, and the signified is the state of affairs together with its qualities and real relations. (Ibid., 45)

In terms of vernacular creativity and slang, then, it is humour that often serves as the 'aleatory points' in conversation, which convey the signified and simple constructions of language where identity is expressed in language. This does present a paradox in that in language signification comes first propositionally as we are born into a language, whereas in the domain of logic the primary proposition put forward by Deleuze is denotation. Deleuze explains this in that 'paradox is initially that which destroys good sense as the only direction, but it also that which destroys common sense as the assignation of fixed identities' (2004, 5). For Deleuze, signification can only occur because denotation allows the following significations to not be true or false; in terms of identity this means that signification can have different meanings for different people and thus a different construction, and this is one of the ways we get fandom-specific slang terms.

The Furries even have a name for part of their vernacular known as 'yiffing' which is a way of talking when engaging in cybersex online. There are specific terms which are only used in the Furry Fandom when Furries engage in cybersex, such as the word 'Murr' which is used to express sexual gratification (Howl 2015; Hypetaph 2015). Furries' use of Furry vernacular in cybersex is very much the same as those engaging in heterosexual or homosexual cybersex. Furries may use extra indications of movement by referring to 'their' ears or tail moving in sexual arousal. This is because, as Alan McKee (2018) notes, fans of porn have agency rather than being passive consumers. So for Furries, the ability to place themselves within their pornography is similar to many other fandoms that also have porn or sex-based vernacular.

Conclusion

In Baym's research on online soap opera communities she found that some of the more revered members were those who gave good advice or those who wrote particularly good fan fiction (2015, 90); in the case of *Doctor Who* fandom, those who are particularly knowledgeable or are old enough to have watched the original series are higher in the fan hierarchy (Booth and Kelly 2013). Therefore, online communities mirror offline communities in that 'codes of practice can only be 'understood' with the aid of this community' (Van de Goor 2015, 278). The above communities have reinforced what they consider makes a person a good member of the habitus. This has, however, led to what most would see as negative behaviour being endorsed as acceptable in certain online communities. When it comes to the act of 'flaming' on message boards, contrary to early opinions in internet research, Baym found that it occurred not due to 'a lack of social norms ... but *because* of social norms' (2015, 66; emphasis in original).[10] This is why some Furries in my study stated that they chose to not reveal being a Furry online, because in some online spaces, it is the social norm to bully people with Furry avatars. Unfortunately, trolls also have developed their own vernacular which is used to discriminate against Furries such as the term 'FurFag'. This is due to the misconception (or perhaps social norm) that trolls have that all Furries are sexual deviants.

The creation of the online identity is not as easy as just 'being yourself'; there are several factors to be considered when crafting this which may affect how an online identity is formed. Creation depends on how much of the self a person believes can be fully immersed in any given situation: Are we the same identity at all in different moments in time? Grant McCracken writes that identity is cultivated from various parts of a person's life:

> We can occupy a range of people, professions, and predicaments, among them
> air batonist, aviator, city planner, and museum creator. We can cultivate several
> versions of the gendered self. (2008, 277)

For Booth, this is because 'formation of identity hinges on the interactive response of others, on the back-and-forth responses of the community' (2010, 164). Creation of an identity is influenced depending on which community they choose to express themselves within. Creation must then also be carefully tailored to that community as 'in most online encounters, others will have fairly limited cues with which to interpret use, and may or may not make of them the meanings intended' (Baym 2015, 135). Identity creation must be learned as coming from the subject themselves. This conforms to the theory of 'self-categorization'. This theory argues that a person at any given time categorizes themselves in terms of either social or personal identity. This theory, boosted by the work by Carlo Perrotta (2009, 42–3) helps to explain why we act differently when with friends (personal identity) than when we are with a group such as work (social identity). Creation of an online identity is also as fluid as in the offline world and thus the creation of the identity and the direction in which it goes can be different depending on where the online identity is being produced.

The subject of several studies has been the idea of the online environment and the possibility to be anonymous has meant that some can create an online identity that they are unable to express in their offline identity due to stigmatization. Janet H. Long and Guoming Chen refer to this as 'role confusion' in which the adoption of a negative identity can lead to a 'successful resolution to their identity crisis' (2007, 100). The word 'confusion' has not been interpreted here as a negative word in that the subject themselves are confused but that their offline and online identities have become blurred. The creation of their identity may mean that some parts of their identity can only be shared in the online space. For Furries, this can mean that they can only be Furries online as they feel they could be stigmatized for showing this identity offline:

> Expressing identity is a strong self-motivator for using the Net. People who feel important aspects of their identity are unexpressed due to fear of a negative reception will often search chat rooms for role relationships in which to engage stigmatized aspects of their identity. (Ibid.)

In online communities where non-heteronormative users are unable to be gay in the offline world, 'testing out honest self-disclosure and expressing ones "real" self online can be empowering and liberating' (Baym 2015, 139). Also, it can mean that those who have issues offline with harmful experiences such as self-harm or anorexia can find a unique and comforting space to express themselves (Perrotta 2009, 42). Nevertheless, even in communities that allow those with stigmatized offline identities to be free to express that identity, it does not mean that there is no conflict and arguments as to what is the 'correct' way to express that identity.

I have argued here that the main place where Furries create their norms of 'being a Furry' is within the online Furry habitus. This is because there is no set text that a Furry can refer to, although they do 'poach' from anthropomorphic cartoons and because geographically many Furries do not live closely to each other (or perhaps do not want to reveal themselves in public due to stigmatization).

The online habitus is not always a safe space for Furries; several different online communities have been accused of enforcing misogyny as a social norm, such as Reddit and 4Chan. There is some evidence to suggest that adolescents who were frequent users of social networking communities experience more psychological distress due to negative reinforcement as well (ibid., 67). This may be because some communities reinforce increased risk-taking or encourage users to cultivate an image of a 'perfect life' leading other users to believe that their connections on Instagram or Facebook, for instance, are happier than they are.[11] Online spaces and fan communities can offer opportunities to be more reflexive, however. Stanfill argues that this is seen more within the younger fan bases who are demographically more likely to use the internet and online fan communities:

> People who have been in fandom for a while, and in several fandoms over time, have been exposed to and/or acculturated into that set of practices and values, but generational turnover is happening in the population that creates fan texts, and from my own limited and anecdotal experience, younger fan bases are often not within the tradition. (Stanfill 2013a)

Even though the process of enculturation suggests that 'newcomers are gradually accepted and socialised through interaction with peers and more experienced members' (Perrotta 2009, 24), so are lurkers who do not interact because they still see visual cues on what behaviour is acceptable. Online fandom fits in with concepts of institutions in that they are 'produced and reproduced in cultural practices' even if they are more fluid and subject to change over time (Whiteman and Metivier 2013, 154). Due to the norms and values associated with particular online communities, the web pages present the observer with visual clues on how to create their online persona in keeping with their chosen community. In conclusion, Furry signifiers are going to be found in the online fan community than elsewhere.

4

Species choice in the Furry Fandom

Dress, and costumes in particular, are wearable art ... costuming and 'dressing-up' enable individuals, particularly men, opportunities to explore and express aspects of identities through animal performance.
                                                    – Satinsky and Green (2016)

Fursona choices

How do we pick an identity? If you look at yourself now, how did you decide that you were going to 'look' a certain way, for instance? You will presumably have a multiple set of reasons, you may have been influenced by an actor or perhaps a music genre; your cultural or religious background; your body type; whether you can physically grow hair or not. But typically, we do not wake up one day and decide that this is how we are going to look like for the rest of our lives; it is usually an ongoing process of negotiation throughout our lifetimes, influenced as we go. As I as well as the IARP have stressed, a fursona is also an identity, an extension and sometimes an improvement on the Furries' own personality and life. But why do they choose certain 'looks' for their fursonas? The IARP have put forward evidence that fursonas are incredibly popular throughout the fandom, but why certain species are co-opted for these identities have not been forthcoming despite data showing correlations that canines are the most popular species to have. The IARP have noted that some species rarely exist at all – primates, for instance, are virtually never chosen, and I found this in my data as well.

In my research sample, canines were the most popular species for fursona use within the fandom. The next most popular category was a species mix, but even in this instance, out of the 133 mixed-species fursonas, 64 were canines mixed with another species. But why are canines so popular? This is something I was very intrigued to find out, especially considering the difference between the choices made by hobbyists and lifestylers.

Hobbyists – companion animal relationships

Although Chapter 3 mapped out various signifiers that are shared between both hobbyist and lifestyler Furries, they have a different way of interpreting the animal itself when they use it for their fursona. Hobbyist Furries are more likely to view their chosen species through a 'companion animal' lens, which is a theory from Haraway (2003) concerning the certain types of animals we bring up from mere non-human status in a humanist hierarchy. Canines and felines are the most commonly used fursonas across the Furry Fandom and it may seem obvious when looking at pet 'ownership' across the world. In Western countries (where many Furries are based) dog or cat ownership is very common.

But the relationship between animals and humans goes far further than the relatively recent history of domestic pet ownership, especially when it comes to dogs and cats. Canines have been the subject of domestication for at least the past 15,000 years, possibly longer (Bradshaw 2011, 31). And although modern dogs look very different from their wolf ancestors, they still share 99.96 per cent of their DNA structure (ibid., 3). Cats too have been the product of domestication, with archaeological evidence being found in China dating between 5,500 and 4,900 BCE revealing the leopard cat (*Prionailurus bengalensis*) being subject to 'domestication' by humans (Vigne et al. 2016, 1). Similar to domesticated canines, the behaviour of cats that led to their domestication is the ability 'to adapt to human modified and cultivated environments' (ibid., 5). Which is a major contributing factor for domestication over other 'untameable' species (ibid., 5).

There is a speciesist issue with tameness when it comes to the animal. There are scientific and evolutionary reasons why some species will not be tamed; cockroaches are disgusted by humans to such a degree that if they are touched by us they run away and then wash themselves.[1] There are also cultural reasons why humans have decided that some species are 'untameable', creating a preference for certain types of dogs, for example, over others. Even if the cockroach did not find us humans disgusting, it has no aesthetic value for speciesist people and so it would be unlikely for anyone to attempt to tame it, thus labelling the animal 'untameable' instead. John T. Maher examines this issue when looking at legal personhood for animals: 'the possibility of an inclusive justice for animals is an illusion as long as humans define species-based ontologies' (2014, 45). The exaltedness of 'tameable' creatures over 'untameable' ones is a symptom of this.

There has been criticism in recent years that many observations of wolves, and then comparisons of these communities to modern dogs, have been flawed. Jacques Derrida and David Willis have noted that these observations do not understand the social communiqué between animal packs as the researchers 'fail to meet the gaze' of the animal (2002, 382). Many dog trainers would look to the wolf to emulate the 'alpha male' status that they believed they needed to make their dog obedient. However, this ontology has mostly come from observations of wolf packs in zoo enclosures, creating artificial aggressive behaviour, whereas in the wild a wolf would depart from its previous pack rather than fight (Bradshaw 2011, 21). Although this would seem to be an anthropocentric perception of 'avoiding a fight', there is evidence of covertly observed wolves producing this avoidance behaviour which has led to a change in the way scholars have looked at 'typical' animal behaviour (ibid., 20).

But it is not just because of our long history of domestication which makes dogs and cats an easy and well-known vessel on which to craft a fursona. As understanding of animal behaviour has changed, so too has humanity's relationship with them. Long gone are the days where cats were important signifiers in religious practices. Ancient examples of cat worship such as anthropomorphization of the Goddesses Bastet and Sekhmet were an example of this.[2] Cat worship has continued in unprecedented ways. In the strange and wonderful world of the internet subcultures, you are just as likely to have a cat ask you whether it 'can has Cheezburger?' or tell you whether it is particularly grumpy that day than a bland conversation about the virtues of cat ownership.[3] The Furry Fandom, as I have noted previously in this book, is well and truly situated in the online space and uses animal memes to communicate such as the Reddit subforum r/furry_irl, where they share memes which lament or celebrate aspects of being a Furry.[4]

There are also psychological rather than cultural reasons as to why using a familiar furry face to create a fursona is so attractive. Studies have shown that our perception of dogs and cats has often been aesthetically driven. In a study on the perception of the physical appearance of dogs, physical attributes such as coloured irises and an 'approximation' of a smile ranked highest when participants looked at doctored pictures of dogs. It was concluded that 'certain physical attributes such as symmetry and averageness, have been demonstrated to influence judgments of attractiveness. ... These preferences can extend to nonhuman, inanimate objects' (Hecht and Horowitz 2015, 153–4). Humans find it easier to anthropomorphize mammals (as they are closer to our taxonomic group) due to their aesthetics creating an emotional reaction which we find familiar – it is much easier to create an aesthetic in Photoshop or in an artwork of a dog smiling than it is a bird (the beak makes this awkward). This may be why Wilkins et al. noted that there is

> [a] significant difference in emotion attribution across all taxonomic categories of animal, with mammals receiving the highest attribution of emotions, followed by birds, reptiles, fish and invertebrates, respectively. (2015, 363)

For hobbyists as well, real-life logistics may come into play when they are choosing their fursona. The number of Furries who wish to own a physical fursuit of their fursona is very high across multiple studies (see Chapter 3), and so, logistically, the fursona that is chosen needs to be something that can be worn.[5] For a fursuit to be wearable, it has to fit around the human body (at least in the present moment) which (in most cases) means space for two legs and two arms. Although many of the most popular species are quadrupeds, a human can still 'wear' the animal by making it bipedal, that is, stand up on two legs when they wear the costume. This could indicate why animals such as snails, snakes and the plethora of other limbless vertebrae are rare, to the extent that I have not seen one in my research yet. This makes sense from a cosplay standpoint as it would be incredibly difficult to create a fursuit, for example, of a fish because a human would not be able to 'wear it'. As noted by Debra

Ferreday, even those only wearing partial fursuit pieces find it important for these pieces to be wearable. When discussing cervine pieces, Ferreday noted that the antlers were 'designed to blend in with the wearer's clothing, look less like trophies taken from dead prey than like prosthetics' (2011, 222). In fact, the very name 'Furry' suggests mammalian species should be chosen, which may suggest why most fursuits are made of furlike materials and why there is a preponderance for furry species being the top fursona choices.

There is also one last important factor as to how hobbyists in particular chose certain species over others and this is because they are being influenced by popular animal media myths. This is important in as much as the Furries are part of a fandom and thus 'poaching' from media texts to incorporate into their fandom is a standard fan practice. Also, Furries' opinions on popular fursona species did not simply come out of autopoiesis because collective understandings of myth about animal species are anthropocentric.[6]

For hundreds of years, animals have retained a special place in myths; the stork, for example, was a symbol of blessing in Roman times; in Italy, they are considered harbingers of good fortune; in Germany and in the Netherlands, a stork resting on a family home is viewed as a good omen. The raven also shares a similar myth across national lines in that in Swedish and Germanic folklore they are considered as representations of damned or lost souls. Similarly, in English, Celtic and Scandinavian traditions they are symbolic of death. For Roland Barthes, 'myth is a system of communication' (1957, 131) and the hobbyists use different animal species as a conduit for these traits; without myths, to tell a Furry 'a lion is brave' or to paraphrase a well-known cartoon advertisement that 'a tiger is great', they would have limited reasons for choosing a species.[7]

A good example of a media text which helps illustrate how we ascribe traits to anthropomorphized animals is the 2016 film *Zootopia* (also known as *Zootropolis*) directed by Bryon Howard.[8] The film did relatively well at the box office and has since become a media text which has been assigned to being a 'Furry' movie by members of the fandom. *Zootopia* is a typical example of animals being anthropomorphized with qualities that have attributed to them from human myth. The first portrayal of crime in the movie is when Judy Hopps (a rabbit) witnesses a con pulled by two foxes, Nick Wilde and his sidekick Finnick. It is no coincidence that foxes have been chosen as these species have long been ascribed the trait of 'cunningness' and being a trickster in tales such as *The Fox and the Stork* (Aesop 620–564 BCE) or *Reynard the Fox* (De Saint Cloud 1170).[9] It would make little sense for Nick Wilde to have been, for example, a donkey which in many stories has been portrayed as stubborn or stupid – Aesop's *The Ass in the Lion's Skin* (620–564 BCE) portrayed donkeys as stupid and so did Shakespeare's popularization of the donkey as an 'ass' in *A Midsummer Night's Dream* (1595–96). The use of a donkey as a con man would not have fit in with popular representations of the anthropomorphic donkey and so it would be seen to not have the 'finesse' to orchestrate such a clever crime.

This hierarchy is seen in *Zootopia*, too, first as a narrative tool. All the animals portrayed in the movie are strictly carnivore or herbivore (no animals which are omnivore in nature) with a clear animated (and narrative) line with characters who are either predator animals or prey. Second, and the most striking point, is that there are no primates in the movie at all. When Byron Howard was asked about what animals would be appearing in the movie, he stated:

> One mammal you won't see is simians or apes. Apes are too much like us, so as soon as we put them in the story, everyone goes, oh the ape is the smart one. And we wanted all these mammals to seem like more or less equal intelligence, more or less. (Frost 2016)

As mentioned in this chapter's introduction, there has never been an explanation as to why apes have not been popular when it comes to anthropomorphization within the Furry Fandom. The similarity between humans and apes is likely to be one of the reasons for this. Furthermore, The Furry Fandom is predominantly a Western phenomenon and for many Furries, they have created their preferred styles of anthropomorphization from interactions within their own culture, a culture which is lacking in myths of apes.

As shown in *Zootopia*, myth is biased in that it has prescribed value on certain species over others. That is not to say that species cannot be positively represented – *Gorillas in the Mist* (Michael Apted 1988) won five academy awards for its sympathetic portrayal of gorillas and how they should be protected. However, these gorillas were not anthropomorphized and the film was meant to shed a positive light on real-life conservation. In recent years, the most popular and commercially successful representation of apes has been in the *Planet of the Apes* franchise (Arthur P. Jacobs 1968–73) with a successful remake (Tim Burton 2001) and then a complete reboot of the franchise in 2011 with *Rise of the Planet of the* Apes (Rupert Wyatt 2011), *Dawn of the Planet of the Apes* (Matt Reeves 2014) and *War of the Planet of the Apes* (Matt Reeves 2017). Although these films were popular among viewers, they do not shed a good light on primates. The film narrative shows the apes destroying most of the human population via simian flu and then later waging war on the last remaining humans. Current myths surrounding primates in Western countries usually take a darker turn when it comes to anthropomorphization, and so their myths are not as inviting as more positive myths about animals in contemporary film.

Another point to consider is that the Furry Fandom is predominantly white and so they may not wish to associate with apes due to racist connotations that have been attributed to apes in the past (whether they knowingly do this or not). For hundreds of years there has been a 'vigorous tradition which linked the Negro with the ape' (Jordan 2012, 32), which Winthrop D. Jordan notes is often due to the sexual connection attributed to the ape:

> The sexual connection between Negro and ape has served to express the deep-seated feeling that the Negro was more animal – and accordingly more sexual – than the white man. (Ibid., 491)

Sara Silah argues that 'race-thinking is a form of speciesism that is highly invested in notions of the animal and the human' (2007, 96). She argues that Haraway is correct in her assumption that primatology has led apes to being coded as representations of Black people by white discourse (1989, 117). For Silah,

> Haraway suggests in her inclusion of 'the obscurity of colour' simian orientalism is a thoroughly racialized discourse, in which the boundaries of a gendered, white western self are secured through the construction of a dark, furry, ape 'other'. (2007, 98)

I agree then that in Western countries, myth about apes often have racist connotations which could perhaps be why many of the white members of the Furry Fandom have not chosen apes as fursonas. Although a researcher could point to *Cujo* (Lewis Teague 1982) as a very negative representation of dog, this film was only a modest financial and mixed critical success.[10] In comparison, there is a huge plethora of positive dog-myth films including, but certainly not limited to, *Air Bud* (Charles Martin Smith 1997) which spawned five movies, seven spin-off movies and two Christmas specials about dogs playing sports and, of course, helping humans through trials and tribulations; eleven movies in the *Lassie* franchise spanning from 1943 to 2005; and *Beethoven* (Brian Levant 1992) also becoming a successful franchise which included its own TV series and seven movies. Additionally, unlike the ape, there are far fewer racial connotations with humans being associated with dogs, although it should be noted that there are sexist examples with women being referred to as bitches.

Lifestylers – post-human identities

One of the main research aims of my work was to present evidence that, unlike previous IARP research implies, the Furries are not a homogenous group. I have argued here that hobbyists are influenced by myth but lifestylers are also moving into the post-human and are subscribing to the process of becoming-animal. This theory by Deleuze and Guattari (as I set out earlier in this book) theorizes that 'a becoming is not a correspondence between relations. But neither is it a resemblance, an imitation, or at the limit, an identification' (2013a, 277). This precludes hobbyists from the process of becoming-animal as many of them in my research cited just 'identifying' with the animal. For those highly identified Furries, their fursona choice is co-opting the animal into their human identity rather than identifying or imitating it. Ferreday likens those who highly identify with a canine fursona to the idea of the werewolf:

> The most visible human/nonhuman trans figure is the werewolf, whose violent transformation from human to animal is often held to embody the expression of an innate animal nature which has been repressed. (2011, 219)

For highly identified Furries, transformation is at the forefront, in that these real animals can transform their human selves. This is also similar to Haraway's notion of the cyborg (1991) and then her later addition of companion species (2003). Haraway now considers the cyborg to be the 'junior siblings in the much bigger, queer family of companion species' (ibid., 11). She also put forward the notion that kin is not just for genealogy: 'My purpose is to make "kin" mean something other/more than entities by ancestry or genealogy ... kin making is making persons, not necessarily as individuals or as humans' (2016, 103). Dogs are at their very essence real, something that is material and can be touched, something that is far easier to envision than the cyborg. Unlike the cyborg, we have been bioengineering dogs through breeding programmes for decades before we even began using artificial technology. Haraway notes that 'optimization does not mean perfection' (1991, 64) and as humanity has strived to create the 'perfect breed' it has sometimes led to unhealthy consequences for the breed itself. Haraway has in the past complained about the work of Deleuze and Guattari unnecessarily pushing aside the generic love of animals from humans as 'mundane' (2008, 27), quoting the phrase from *A Thousand Plateaus* that 'anyone who likes cats or dogs is a fool' (2013a, 281). However, these theorist's bodies of work complement each other surprisingly well together in discussions on the Furry Fandom. This is despite the fact that Haraway has been criticized for her selective use of citations from *A Thousand Plateaus* (Stivale 2014, 76). This is because, as suggested by Joanna Bednarek, 'it is worth mentioning here that the source of [Haraway's] bias is the fact that she has different premises and priorities than the authors of *A Thousand Plateaus*' (2017, 56). Haraway's critique of Deleuze and Guattari's attitude to animals is because she suggests that they are taking a speciesist approach towards them; however, I am inclined to use the interpretation of Bednarek:

> The negative attitude towards dogs and cats touches here only on the cultural meanings associated with them; the role fulfilled by actual animals depends on the case, that is, on the way they function in the assemblage. (Ibid., 54)

When Haraway asks, 'what do feral cats have to do with community college students?' (2008, 281) the question is reminiscent of Deleuze's work on Lewis Caroll whose famous conundrum asks, 'Why is a raven like a writing desk?'

(Carroll 1865). Her answer is that 'both classes of beings are being "educated" through their intra-actions within historically situated technology' (2008, 281), an idea that is echoed through most of Deleuze and Guattari's teachings. Animals and how they are represented are important in that 'for Deleuze, the animal has a privileged and very specific relation to the notions of territory and world, one that is based on a relative number of affects and on a process of selections' (Lambert 2017, 255). Like becoming, understanding the body is much deeper than understanding the simple relation between 'tongue making you talk' and the simple fact that you have 'legs with which you walk', there must be an understanding of why humans do not 'sing with your sinuses' as they suggest (Deleuze and Guattari 2013a, 175). A BwO is looking far beyond the simple functions of the body and, as such, an organ is nothing by itself, it only becomes useful when it has a purpose on the planes of consistency with other functions. Going back to the feral cat and college students, both are assigned numbers for tracking purposes and both are required to get vaccinations (Haraway 2008, 281). Both are thrown into a new place where they do not know anybody and so could be considered as the same body if you were considering them as just that, a body. Haraway, Deleuze and Guattari have all noted a crucial aspect of the post-human, which is the interaction between our nature and how it can be profoundly altered by how we interact with our environment (much like the feral cat and the college student). In this case, technology *and* the body are shaped by this environment. It is imperative to look at the assemblages to find out how the feral cat or the college student *become* a feral cat or a college student rather than just assuming that they came to be simply because they are: 'In short, symbolic understanding replaces the analogy of proportion with an analogy of proportionality' (Deleuze and Guattari 2013a, 276). This can be applied to the understanding of species choice in the Furry Fandom.

If you strip a Furry out of their fursuits and fursonas and are just presented with the naked body, they become simply that – a body. Their identity of the lifestyler Furry cannot be represented through the simple means of their actions or words which come from the body but from their identifying of Furry signifiers. For Therians, Grivell et al. (2014) used a definition that 'a person who is, feels, or believes he/she is in part or whole (non-physically) one or more non-human animals on an integral, personal level' (ibid., 115). This would be in keeping with Deleuze and Guattari in that this splinter group from Furries is not imitating the animal but has been produced through filiation. This would also be in keeping with Haraway. The animal has been incorporated by optimizing their identity as non-human or ahuman rather than a speciesist approach valuing their human identity more than their animal identity.

A post-human use of the animal has been important in postmodern art and I argue here that the use of the animal by lifestylers in their fursona species choice directly correlates with this. The animal has been used as a metaphor for postmodern artists for varying reasons, some of which aim to 'cast the fixity of identity as an inhibition of creativity' (Baker 2000, 18). It has been in this way that they 'consider new forms of existence' (Thompson 2005, 9). Considering new forms of existence is prominent in lifestylers; in the data collected for this book, respondents explained that creating a new identity for themselves using an animal as a template was a way to improve. As well as this, my research showed that in most instances a fursona would change as the Furries' identity changed – it was not static and as identities can change throughout a person's life, it follows that the animal with which they chose to incorporate can also change.

For postmodern artists, keeping the form of the animal is a mark of 'respect for the otherness of the animal' (Baker 2000, 96), and this is seen widely in Furry artwork. Fursonas keep the form of the chosen species sometimes with added extras such as clothing or colour changes. For postmodern artists 'becoming-animal' is about 'draw[ing] the animal in' (ibid., 134) and this is the intention behind 'becoming-animal' for Deleuze and Guattari as well. 'Drawing the animal in' is meant in the sense that the animal is incorporated into the identity rather than used in a hierarchical structure. The animal is just as important to their identity as their humanness because it has been anthropomorphized and thus on a level par with the human part of the identity as they have 'assimilated'. This is why lifestylers, as studied by the IARP (without using the term to distinguish them from less identified Furries) often see the fursona as 'integral' to their identity. This may be why challenges to how much they see their fursona as a part of their identity can cause 'additional discrimination' (Roberts et al. 2015b, 47).

Unfortunately, members of the Furry Fandom not only suffer stigmatization from the media but have also been stigmatized by postmodern artists and academics. Authors such as Baker write intelligently on the way postmodern artists use anthropomorphism in artwork, but there is a clear indication that he had not thoroughly considered fans of anthropomorphization, such as the Furries in his work. In fact, Furries are reduced to a mere sentence when he is describing the 'understandable' desire for the proper artists to not be associated with:

> The bizarre goings-on of the people who now call themselves 'Furries', spend their lives dressed as cuddly animals and whose fantasies 'sometimes extend to actual bestiality' which they are keen to discuss on a growing number of internet sites. (cited in Baker 2000, 172)[11]

This violent reaction to human becoming animal is succinctly summarized by philosopher Simon Critchley, who noted that 'there is something charming about an animal become human' but goes on to state that 'when the human becomes animal, then the effect is disgusting' (Cox 2005, 19). This may be because there is seemingly a bias from some artists about what is considered high art or low art. For some, high art should be considered as 'real art' because it requires 'active spectatorship' compared to popular/mass art which generates 'broad appeal and accessibility' making it formulaic and passive (Fisher 2005, 533). At a glance, fursona art may be seen to contain these 'low art' qualities as they do have mass appeal with the cute, Disney-like aesthetics. However, persons such as Baker, who have only heard negative stereotypes about Furries and thus do not understand the identity construction a fursona entails, and do not understand the active participation that Furries can often have with their fursonas.

Another reason why people (as well as artists) may be hostile to Furries is that they may also have prejudices that have been consigned to certain 'kinds' of animals and also certain 'kinds' of humans. For Carol Adams,

> While it goes without saying that 'humans are animals' the way this insight has been used has been hierarchically, i.e., racial and sexual distinctions were used to equate people of color and women with other animals or to impute animal characteristics on those who were not white, propertied men. 'Human' became

a definition not only about humans versus (other) animals, but also defining who among Homo sapiens would have the power to act as 'humans'. (2006, 120)

For Marla Carlson it is because lifestylers inhabit an identity which is post-human in that it challenges what is typically 'human'. When writing about the Furries, she also uses Haraway to suggest why their identity is put at the bottom of hierarchies: 'Like the cyborg and the animal, the freak performer inhabits the borders of the Human – and that is why these categories exist, because they bracket off varieties of life in order to define humanity' (Carlson 2011, 199).

Lifestylers are incorporating the animal into their own identity in such a successful way that they have the empathy to draw becoming-animal into reality. This is also similar to the way that Ferreday views Furries with cervine fursonas: 'It is more useful, I think, to think in terms of what the longing to become deer, always imagined as a *partial* becoming, might tell us about the ways in which boundaries of the human are constructed and maintained' (2011, 222). This is why postmodern artists have failed to take the Furry Fandom seriously. That is not to say that Furries use animal species in the same way as postmodern artists as it is argued here that they do not, but, Furries and postmodern artists use animals in different ways for the same purpose, for becoming-animal. This is reinforced by my research which found that lifestylers had a far greater connection with their fursona species compared to hobbyists, who often cited aesthetic reasons for choosing or changing their fursona compared to lifestylers who choose or changed their fursona due to personality changes within themselves.

Conclusion

Species choice is very important when it comes to the Furry Fandom and I have argued here that it is not a natural one. Instead, hobbyists are influenced primarily by myth and that lifestylers then take this further to produce a post-human relationship with their fursona. It is unsurprising when considering the theory by Haraway and others that companion animals dominate popular Furry species of choice, and that animals which are often 'meat' (bovines, swines, fowl) are rare.

There will be proponents of this who will argue that this is a negative conclusion. Essentially because this conclusion could be construed as saying that either hobbyists or lifestylers are not complicit in the animals they choose but have been forced into choosing certain animals via culture. However, the very point of post-humanism and 'becoming-animal' is that it is not a 'natural' process in the way society would want us to behave. In their discussions on 'becomings' in a *Thousand Plateaus*, they are described as the 'process of mimesis [that] brings nature and culture together' (Deleuze and Guattari 2013a, 275). The Jungian and demonic archetypes are important to consider with the highly identified Furries in the Furry Fandom as they suggest *becoming* rather than *imitating* the literal animal; resisting the Oedipal structure and thus launching a becoming-animal.

A human will see a lion, a predator, almost silently sneak up on a gazelle before it strikes it down. The human seeing this anthropomorphizes the animal to explain the chain of events – the lion 'sneaking' up on the gazelle as cunning and the killing of the gazelle as powerful traits that many humans would like to emulate themselves. The proposition as to whether the lion knew it was being 'cunning' by sneaking up on the gazelle does not matter as there is no true or false interpretation of the Jungian archetype. Therefore, it does not matter whether an animal 'truly' has the traits that have been ascribed to it by humans as the signification of the character trait ascribed becomes more important than mere truth. Only when the subject has moved away from the traditional and into the cyborg culture does this happen. As MacCormack argues,

> Commonality can be interpreted not as resemblance but by an openness of each element to experiencing the other as self and thus self as other, 'now rejecting this way of defining by kind and specific difference'. (2014, 2)

Again, it is necessary to see non-humans as more 'tactical' in categorization so as to not restrict the analysis of Furry myth into a moral duality (ibid., 6). It can be argued that there is no reason why animals could not have both negative and positive traits, because ultimately these are human perceptions which do not represent the 'real' animal. And, although animals are signified sometimes in a negative way in myth, that does not necessarily transcribe over into people's real-life knowledge and feelings on the animal. It could simply be a useful narrative tool. This does, however, mean that different species have been given varying levels of importance depending on which culture (geographically) the myth has appeared in. For Lévi-Strauss it was extremely important to look at why these differences occur between similar myths (1978, 31) as it gives an indication to why certain animals are higher in this speciesist hierarchy. For example, in *Structural Anthropology 2* (Lévi-Strauss 1976), the function and nature of an owl changes from clan to clan in old Native American myth. One myth describing the owl as a ruthless killer who stole children to eat them compared to a different tribe's myth which had the owl stealing women in which to make them his wife. This is due to the differences in real life about whether rivalling tribes would primarily steal members of other tribes or kill them.

Furries choose animals because of their affinity with them – much like Haraway would argue that women had an affinity with using the internet as it was a space where they could explore identity away from the oppressive nature of patriarchy. Furries are able to do this by way of species choice; by playing with the very nature of the animal, they are able to create their companion species. For hobbyists, their affinity comes from the way they can play with aesthetics with animals that are familiar to them, and for lifestylers, their affinity comes from a post-human connection with the animal.

Although there may be an Orwellian sense of 'all animals are equal, but some animals are more equal than others', much quoted from *Animal Farm* (1945), I believe this is not a negative judgement that has been made by Furries, but they have simply judged some species as 'better' for incorporation. Furries are still very much human and so they cannot be judged too harshly for incorporating animals that are familiar and aesthetically pleasing for 'becoming-animal'. Maybe in the future this will evolve into different species but for now companion animals reign supreme in the Furry world but not for the reason of simple affinity and geographical closeness that has been suggested in studies so far.

It can be argued that for Haraway, companion animals tend to get a favoured status, thus remaining Oedipalized, that of comfort and sitting at their masters' feet rather than species on a par with humanity. In her recent work, she invokes the image of Cthulhu and its tentacles to describe the ways in which we, humans and non-humans, are all connected:

> The tentacular are also nets and networks, IT critters, in and out of clouds. Tentacularity is about life lived along lines – and such a wealth of lines – not at points, not in spheres 'The inhabitants of the world, creatures of all kinds, human and non-human, are wayfarers'; generations are like 'a series of interlaced trails'. String figures all. (2016, 32)

She invokes the idea of string figure games and their similarities with tentacles, and how the string figures become more and more connected and mixed up the longer the game continues. Using Haraway and tentacular ideas is important for myth as it represents a post-human framework for how myth transfuses across these lines – not being influenced from a human/non-human hierarchy as previous theories suggest. For the Furry Fandom this is important because they do not have a set media text and so it is not one myth (or canon) being passed between Furries when it comes to species choice but myths shifting from all different areas.

Species choice, when it comes to fursonas in the Furry Fandom, are well and truly in the post-human sphere for lifestylers, as they exhibit the signifiers mentioned by Haraway and Deleuze and Guattari. Therians claim that their identity includes shifting mentally into that animal state, such as 'feeling their tail wagging' (Grivell et al. 2014, 115) and this has led some people to label them with a mental illness (ibid., 113). Although not speaking about Furries or Therians specifically, Deleuze and Guattari predicted psychoanalysis would become a terrible thing for those 'becoming-animal' as many would be pathologized. Lifestylers have been pathologized in their post-human experience with their fursonas as it has been reduced to fetishism or masochism, even gaining scorn from hobbyists. This has unfortunately been the way of many parts of post-humanism which have pushed beyond the organic concepts of the body and into the cyber world and why I found it an important aspect to address in the next chapter of this book.

5

Stigmatization in the Furry Fandom

The furry fandom is often the target of significant stigmatization. ...
Stigmatization of the furry fandom is due, in part, to negative portrayals of the
fandom in the media, which has tended to portray furries as sexual deviants.
– Reysen et al. (2015a)

The relationship between identity and stigma

This chapter looks at how perceived stigmatization has affected identity construction and what this has meant for the Furry Fandom. For the IARP, much of their work has focused on highly identified Furries, and as their research has shown, highly identified individuals are often at more risk of suffering from the effects of stigmatization in minority groups. However, as I have stressed a number of times in this book, not all Furries are alike in their experiences and this includes stigmatization. Therefore, I reject the notion from the IARP research that the vast majority of Furries are stigmatized due to the split between hobbyists and lifestylers; hobbyists with no fursona, for example, feel less stigmatized than lifestylers who are more connected with their fursona and are more heavily involved with the fandom.

Stigma is an associated characteristic or stereotype that resides in a social context. Oppression and prejudice are what come after a stigma has been established in the social setting. Much has been written about the effects that stigmatization can have on both group settings and on an individual level (Alexander 2004; Smelser 2004). Scholars have shown that stigmatization can greatly affect identity construction on both macro and micro scale (Harper 2009; Thio 2010). Although many people can be stigmatized by others expressing prejudice, this does not always become traumatic for them or affect their identity personally or with their group on a cultural level. There have to be special circumstances for an event or traumatic occurrence to leave a permanent mark on the psyche. For Alexander (2004), cultural trauma (and thus a stigmatizing event) only occurs when

> members of a collective feel they have been subjected to a horrendous event that leaves indelible marks upon their group consciousness, marking their memories forever and changing their future identity in fundamental and irrevocable ways. (Ibid., 1)

Alexander argues that it is not the event itself that causes the collective trauma but what happens afterwards with the 'socially mediated attribution' that makes it so (ibid., 8). This may seem counter-intuitive as without the event there would be no trauma at all, but Smelser describes this effect as 'trauma event plus context' (2004, 34). For example, the Black community in America is a stigmatized community because the 'event' of their enslavement before the American Civil War has the 'context' that they are still the targets of brutality and discrimination and frequently the target of political rhetoric today; thus, by using traumatic event plus context, we can pinpoint various events which have caused trauma to Furries perpetuated by the media. The event that first saw Furries experience socially mediated trauma was an episode on television that portrayed them as sexual deviants; the trauma further developed due to sustained bullying experienced by members after this portrayal. Another event + context was when Furries were attacked by chlorine gas at a convention in 2014 (the event). The trauma was established through context when MSNBC reporter Mika Brzezinski ran off the set laughing at the fact that this had happened (see Chapter 2). Additionally, there was a perceived lack of coverage on other major news outlets for such a serious incident. These examples show how the 'socially mediated attribution' theory of Alexander (2004) makes these events a cultural trauma.

Furries as a fandom do suffer from stigmatizing effects due to media coverage. However, it is important to investigate *how much* a Furry is stigmatized on an individual level. Distinguishing between group and individual experiences has been stressed by Leanne Son Hing when researching the effects of physical health in stigmatized people. Son Hing argues that supposedly weak correlations between stigmatization and actual health have only appeared that way due to methodological failures in the studies conducted and that there is actually stronger links between the two (2012, 149). Son Hing discusses the difference in life expectancy between African Americans and white Americans, the average life expectancy of an African American male being six years less than that of a white American male (ibid., 151). The work by Sidanius and Pratto (2001) was noted by Son Hing as one of the few studies (at the time of her writing in 2012) focusing on the connection between stigmatization and physical health. They theorized that because of the disadvantages that African Americans face as a stigmatized group, they tend to have more stressful and dangerous employment and they have less access to quality healthcare. They surmised that this comes from being stigmatized because of their race and that this eventually affects their physical health (Sidanius and Pratto 2001).

Newer research on obesity and stigmatization seem to support the study of Sidanius and Pratto and Son Hing that physical health can be affected by stigmatization. In recent studies, it was found that obese people are stigmatized by people who believe that obesity was in the obese person's control and this led to obese persons being more likely to blame themselves for their condition. This has led to them having worse health as a result, and studies have shown that obese people have an increased risk of depression, isolation, social withdrawal, negative body image, and, counter-intuitively, to binge-eat (Bannon et al. 2009, 118). This, in turn, affected the obese person's physical health. The studies suggest that if a participant is aware of the stereotype about them, this can affect their performance negatively – for example, a woman is told she will not do well on a maths test simply because of the stereotype that 'women are bad at maths' or a Black person is told they will not do well on an intelligence test because 'Blacks are less intelligent than whites'. This indicates that a participant gets so worried about confirming this stereotype that they perform badly due to the stress.[1] It is not, then, surprising that an obese person in the Bannon et al. study reaffirms this stereotype that obese people binge-eat. However, there has also been work on how individuals can combat these negative effects of stigmatization, investigating ways to strengthen their own identity and increase their mental well-being. This is done by changing the context of their 'negative' stereotype and how it relates to their individual identity. Members of the Furry Fandom who consider themselves to have a non-heteronormative identity perform some of these actions.

The article 'Coming Out in the Gay World' (1975) was one of the first to explore how people transition into a homosexual identity rather than the previous works which focused on the 'learning' of homosexual behaviour (Dank 1975, 215). Written at a time where homosexuality had been decriminalized in Britain for less than a decade, he noticed that to improve their well-being many gay men had to recontextualize certain words. They did this by placing themselves in a context where being a gay man was not a negative trait in what he called 'neutralization':

> The meaning of the category must be changed because the subject learned the negative stereotype of the homosexual held by most heterosexuals, and he knows that he is no queer, pervert, dirty old man, and so on. (Ibid., 224)

By doing this he theorized that

> 'I am homosexual, not mentally ill.' The cognitive category of homosexual now becomes socially acceptable, and the subject can place himself in that category and yet preserve a sense of his self-esteem or self-worth. (Ibid., 225)

This neutralization can mean, however, that the homosexual (or a member of other stigmatized groups) no longer identifies with their group for self-preservation reasons. In a study by Major et al. (2003), it was found that Latino Americans who had a strong in-group identification were more depressed than Latinos who did not identify much with the community. In that study, Latinos who found prejudice towards Latinos worrying but did not have a strong in-group identification were able to psychologically separate themselves from the 'Latinos who were being discriminated against'. This mindset can have negative effects when an individual in a stigmatized group begins to blame or scapegoat other members of their group (Smelser 2004, 45–7). This has also been found in the Furry Fandom where hobbyists can become aggressive towards those who see it as a part of their identity, that is, the lifestylers. Stanfill saw this trend when investigating other fandoms:

> Members of non-normative groups will subdivide their group into (a) themselves
> and others like them, whom they classify as normal, and (b) a deviant subgroup
> they declare actually deserves the stigma or pathologization to which the entire
> group is subjected. (2013a, 121)

In the Furry Fandom, this group split is because of the difference in experience between different Furries. This is because construction of identity is often learned 'when socio-cultural activities are significant to the identities of those involved, that is, when they resonate with the living dimension of actual experience (what is relevant for whom).' (Perrotta 2009, 24). Some lifestyler Furries feel that they have a real spiritual connection with animals, especially Therians who sometimes believe that they have an animal soul in the wrong body (Grivell et al. 2014, 119). Hobbyist Furries do not share this lived experience.

Stigmatization or the Furry-specific vernacular term 'fursecution' is a worry within the Furry Fandom that seems to come up often in the IARP research.[2] Research on stigmatized communities suggests that identification with one's stigmatized minority group can be positively related to well-being (Branscombe et al. 1999; Plante et al. 2014, 4). However, on an individual level, stigmatized members may choose to conceal their community status which can have taxing and harmful psychological effects on the individual (Plante et al. 2014). Their Furry-specific work uses social identity theory as its basis: 'the theory posits that people strive to maintain positive and distinct social identities' and, 'that ingroup members use features of intergroup contexts to direct their behaviour when forming a social identity' (ibid., 5). Plante et al. made two interesting findings in their research – that 'members of stigmatized groups were less likely to identify with their group when group boundaries were more permeable' (ibid.) and that they would identify more with their groups if the status within each group was unstable. However, the study suggests that a stigmatized member would identify with the group if it was clear what they are being stigmatized for, but they also needed to know that they could move hierarchically within them. These results supported the hypothesis of Plante et al. that Furries do use concealment strategies to cope with 'anticipated stigmatization due to perceived intergroup status differences' (2014, 13). Plante et al. suggest that using a concealment strategy was a way for a Furry to mediate 'between "Furries", in the perception of socio-structural characteristics of intergroup status differences and self-esteem' (ibid).

The IARP also looked into whether stigmatized groups react to 'distinctiveness threats by endorsing essentialism – the belief that group members share an immutable essence' (Plante et al. 2015, 359). Studies have suggested that people's desire for acceptance means they would rather identify with a stigmatized but distinct minority than with an accepted majority (Plante et al. 2015).[3] They note that studies have shown that there is a difference in the way members of stigmatized groups perceive threats. Less identified members are usually less defensive when it comes to threats while 'highly identified group members, in contrast, are motivated to preserve their group's distinctiveness' (ibid., 360). The Plante et al. study thus hypothesized that highly identified members of a group usually revert to their community when facing stigmatization as seen in other studies (Branscombe et al. 1999; Plante et al. 2014, 4). Therefore, the Furries would also do this and 'strategically endorse essentialist beliefs about the group' (Plante et al. 2015, 361).

To test their hypothesis when it came to a distinctiveness threat, the researchers chose to compare the Furries with the anime fandom as they believe that 'there exists considerable overlap' between them (ibid., 361). However, their reasoning for this is simply that both fandoms interests 'also manifest themselves through artwork and costuming' (ibid.). To me, it seems like a gross oversimplification of the two fandoms. By this argument, if they are similar only via artwork and costuming then the Furry Fandom is facing distinctiveness threats from every media-based fandom. According to other research by the IARP, a huge proportion of Furries have a fursona (Reysen et al. 2015b, 93). In the anime fandom, although fans often identify with anime characters such as the idea of having a 'waifu', they do not usually create anime personas of themselves like Furries do.[4] Their results showed that Furries perceived themselves as distinct from anime fans (and sports fans which was their control group). They found that 'although participants considered sports fans to be more distinct from Furries than anime fans, ratings did not differ significantly across conditions' (Plante et al. 2015, 363). This study did find that highly identified Furries held 'greater essentialist beliefs' because highly identified Furries perceived themselves as stigmatized (ibid., 365). This may be because one of the things that the anime fandom does share comparatively with the Furry Fandom is how it is stigmatized by the mass media. Negative representations portray boys who like anime as paedophiles and sexual deviants, much like how the Furry Fandom is portrayed.

This chapter looks at how perceived stigmatization has affected identity construction and what this has meant for the Furry Fandom. This is framed by Deleuze and Guattari's concepts of the BwO and how cultural schizophrenia can affect stigmatized individuals. This chapter addresses a literature gap in the current work on stigmatization that has been carried out by the IARP. Much of their work has focused on highly identified Furries, and as research has shown, highly identified individuals are often at more risk of suffering from the effects of stigmatization in minority groups. I must emphasize that those with no fursona felt less stigmatized than those who were more heavily involved with the fandom. This is at odds with research by the IARP which does not distinguish clearly between highly identified and less identified Furries, seeing them as a homogenous group, and thus proclaiming all Furries to be similarly stigmatized.

Studying stigmatization can be a difficult subject not only because of the differences that are found on a macro to micro scale but also because of the widely varying coping mechanisms. Although it may seem that this is not a valuable research area, I would agree with Son Hing that 'such a conclusion would be erroneous' (2012, 153). This is because weak effects over time can create and influence larger phenomenon. The following sections in this chapter will thus discuss Furries as both a group and as an individual because by looking at both frameworks we can get a clear picture of why Furries feel stigmatized. I identify two forms of stigmatization that a Furry (whether a hobbyist or lifestyler) may face – the first being outside source, the media, and the second being an internal source, hobbyist versus lifestylers.

Media stigma towards the Furry Fandom

One of the most prolific cases on Furry Fandom presentation in popular media has been the *CSI: Crime Scene Investigation* episode entitled 'Fur and Loathing in Las Vegas' (see Chapter 2), which was first broadcast on 30 October 2003. Ahead of the airing of the episode, producers of the show approached a Furry named Sabre Fox who was then head of the Southern California Furries Yahoo network. After being shown a copy of the script, Sabre Fox expressed his concerns that Furry conventions were just being portrayed as sex orgies in animal costumes and nothing more. Sabre Fox was told by the producers that the show would go on with no changes to the original script. For the members of the Furry Fandom, the release of an episode which made them look like sexual deviants made them feel stigmatized and laughed at by the outside community.

The episode begins with a woman driving late at night and having to swerve to avoid a Furry dressed in a full racoon fur suit. She unfortunately ends up driving head-on into a semi-truck, causing a crash which leads to her death. The CSI team arrives to investigate the dead woman's accident and finds animal footprints leading to the corpse of the Furry. When the pathologist arrives, he seems disturbed at the dead racoon character due to his childhood love of a cartoon racoon called 'Stripey'. This seems inconsistent with a show which often celebrates lack of emotion as scientific distance.

Presentation of the Furry (it is late in the episode when we find out his name is Robert Pitt) as the 'Other' is consistent throughout the episode. Character Warrick Brown (Gary Dourdan) states to Catherine Willows (Marg Helgenberger) that 'if I had to walk around like Rocky Racoon, I'd be drinking too'. When it turns out the man had not been drinking, the pathologist casually states that 'your manimal died sober'. The show devalues the Furry further by adhering to stereotypes commonly associated with the Furry Fandom.[5] Robert Pitt was a computer programmer and also filled the 'nerdy fan' trope of having no family or friends.

The producers show that they have done no real research on what fursuits look like as one scene had an ape suit (as discussed in previous chapters, Furries are very rarely primates) and many of the costumes look like Halloween costumes rather than fursuits. The only character who defends the fandom is Gil Grissom (William Petersen) likening their involvement with the fandom to the Jungian archetype, or like the connection that Native Americans have with spirit animals.[6] At one point, Catherine Willows, after finding semen on a fursuit that has been seized as evidence, states, 'But humping in an animal suit? Whatever happened to normal sex?' Grissom replies with the Freudian notion that no sex is the only unnatural state of sexual arousal, once again being the only character not to 'Other' the Furries.

The episode has a preoccupation with Furries going to conventions for the purposes of sexual gratification as when they first walk into PAFcon (Plushies and Furries Convention) they walk into a room full of people scratching each other sexually, known as scritching. They later see one of their suspects, a cat called Sexy, in a fashion show wearing a skimpy bikini over their fursuit. A later scene reveals that Sexy the cat is actually Bud, a balding middle-aged man, who admits that 'if I don't have my costume on, I pretty much can't get yiffed' – This establishes Furries as being deviant with the episode inferring that Furries are unable to get sex from 'real' people.

The conclusion of the episode is that Robert Pitt's death was actually a tragic accident and that while he was being sick at the side of the road, he was shot by a ranger who thought he was a coyote. This led him running out into the road for help and getting hit by the woman in her car. When discussing the unlikelihood of these events occurring with Captain Jim Brass (Paul Guilfoyle), the fate of the ranger is also spoken of: there will be no charges brought against him even though he killed a human being.

After the show, a range of points were raised inside the Furry Fandom. Some Furries were amused by the portrayal and others found it insulting or misinformed to the point that they were not bothered by the content. Around the time of airing, fandom member KinkyTurtle wrote:

> Perhaps the silliest thing about the show was the PAFcon schedule as it was full of lectures rather than events that usually take place at a convention like art panels; They also made the point that providing breakfast, lunch and dinner for all attendees was a bit of a stretch! (*LiveJournal* 2003)

There were also those who did not blame the producers for wanting to 'sex up' the action for a better story, with popular Furry novelist and artist Ursula Vernon stating,

> I really don't blame the show for taking the weirdest possible angle, because if I were writing the show, I'd do it too. Why? Because a bunch of weirdos in

costumes writhing around to porno music is waaaaay better for the ratings than an hour of slightly geeky people in T-shirts with wolves on them arguing about whether the Lion King was a better movie than Watership Down. (WikiFur 2017)

However, aside from these more conciliatory opinions on the episode, its perceived damage to the fandom's image is still mentioned by Furries today. In an interview with one respondent for this book, he mentioned the show specifically as the beginning of media attention on the Furry Fandom:

Furry Respondent:	[00:41:32] But, the whole, sort of, media attention on the Furry Fandom started some time in the 1990s, early 2000.
Interviewer:	[00:41:41] Yes.
Respondent:	[00:41:41] One of the earliest ones, there was an episode of *CSI*.
Interviewer:	[00:41:45] Fur and Loathing, yes, I've seen it.
Respondent:	[00:41:48] And that, sort of … and, there were all sorts of things around that point, there was a couple of other shows that went into it. And, all of them portrayed us as entirely sexual deviants.
Interviewer:	[00:42:01] Yes.
Respondent:	[00:42:04] And, that's a lot of the media. The thing is, with media, harassing normal people who are just enjoying interests, doesn't sell newspapers or make good viewing.
Interviewer:	[00:42:17] Yes.
Respondent:	[00:42:18] So, they want us to be freaks, and so they will only report on us being freaks. The people who are Furries who aren't … who are relatively hostile to Furries actually displaying this, are people who are desperately trying to not give the media any fodder against us.

This episode of *CSI* is still being mentioned over a decade after it aired because it had a profound effect on the way that Furries perceived the media and outsiders' view upon them. Not only was the episode brought up multiple times in my research data collection, there were a considerable proportion of respondents (83 per cent) who felt that the Furries are portrayed negatively by the media in general. This echoes sentiments in other studies by the IARP (Gerbasi et al. 2008; Plante et al. 2014).

In the study of Roberts et al. (2015b), many of their participants argued they would be uncomfortable with raising their status with a clinician.[7] In the data collected for this book, there were 23 per cent of respondents who would not disclose their Furry Fandom participation to anyone and only 20 per cent would to their family. This is in line with the IARP research which has suggested that up to 90 per cent of Furries selectively disclose their identity due to fear of stigmatization (Roberts et al. 2015b, 47). And one Furry in my study summed up just how bad these representations are to the fandom:

> Furry: The hate really isn't as bad as a lot of people make it out to be. The problem is when someone is not fully/correctly educated on it. For instance: *CSI & 1000 ways to die:* fuck those 'Furry' representations.[8] Sure, there are people who look at the porn (sure, I have, too), but it's really not about that at all, that's just a side effect of any fandom, really (there's a reason rule34 holds so well). I really hate it when something bad happens to a furry, and nobody really takes it seriously (see: MFF2014 evacuation. Plenty of news anchors were just laughing at the fact that someone had tried to kill, or at least seriously injure, a whole bunch of people. But other than that event: good luck finding reputable sources on other furcon evacuations. Sometimes it's just a vine, or a short youtube clip, or a footnote in a blogpost.). We're basically seen as inhuman because either: it's not something they see everyday, so they're just kinda shocked, or they equate Furry to beastiality. You basically have to either have thick skin, or be good at building a big 'ol metaphorical pillow fort around yourself to last in this fandom.

Having to create 'a thick skin' implies that there are elements of the Furry identity that they feel they are supposed to be ashamed of. For Eve Sedgwick, this can be one of the defining problems of identity construction as a minority (2003, 64). She suggests that it is often paranoia about deviant activity from outsiders that causes problems, 'Simply put, paranoia tends to be contagious' (ibid., 126). Due to the stereotypes put out by the examples as mentioned by the Furry respondent above (*CSI* and *1000 Ways to Die*), Furries may feel that paranoia has been induced about their identity by the media. For McCracken,

> In a world that conforms to the theories of George Herbert Mead, identity is ratified by what the individual sees in the mirror of other peoples' reactions. The individual knows herself as she is known by others. (2008, 282)

So, for Furries who see the horror of those who have watched the *CSI* episode dedicated to the deviancy of the Furry Fandom; or those who have read a *Vanity Fair* piece which labelled all Furries as nerds with glasses who were molested (Gurley 2001), it is unsurprising that many Furries then look at their own identity as something to be concealed. However, this stigmatization is worse for those who are lifestylers than it is for hobbyists as the next section will evidence.

Differences in stigma between hobbyists and lifestylers

The IARP almost exclusively speak about the highly identified Furries in terms of 'coming out' about their identity. Due to this, looking at how non-heteronormative identities can be stigmatized and its effects on individuals can be is useful, but only when discussing those who are highly identified Furries. This is because hobbyists are fans who, while vulnerable to bullying, are not inherently in the realm of 'stigma' as those who are playing with a post-human identity as the lifestylers often are.

This may be in part due to the concept of faciality as put forward first by Deleuze before developing further with Guattari. The face represents a political polemic, in that contemporary media often infers certain powers on different kinds of faces. For Deleuze, particularly in *Francis Bacon: The Logic of Sensation* (2003), it is important to see the face as an abstraction:

> Sensation has one face turned toward the subject (the nervous system, vital movement, 'instinct', 'temperament' a whole vocabulary common to both Naturalism and Cezanne) and one face turned toward the object (the 'fact', the place, the event). Or rather, it has no faces at all, it is both things indissolubly. ... And at the limit, it is the same body which, being both subject and object, gives and receives the sensation. (Ibid., 34–5)

For lifestylers, faciality has been used in a negative way by the contemporary media. This may be because they are 'confusing' the 'acceptable' usage of the face. Deleuze noted in the work by Francis Bacon that Bacon's portraits where the face has melded in the body makes faciality fractured. Deleuze argued that previous importance of the head (as figure-head) becomes simply meat in Bacon's work (ibid., 26). As the Furries misplace the figure-head in their artwork by creating becoming-animal, they also displace faciality. Deleuze and Guattari argue that faciality is a process whereby a face is shown to conform to the dominant standards of society:

> Faces are not basically individual; they define zones of frequency or probability … the form of subjectivity, whether consciousness or passion, would remain absolutely empty if faces not form loci of resonance that select the sensed and mental reality and make it conform in advance to a dominant reality. (Deleuze and Guattari 2013a, 196)

A Furry wearing a fursuit head displaces the human head in this way and becomes an empty signifier for a non-Furry. For Furries then, they are still trapped with negative connotations to their different masks in faciality and so mainstreaming has been much harder for their fandom as they are 'less palatable' due to their schizo BwO.

To explain these categories further, Deleuze and Guattari believe that different modes of the body are enacted as follows:

- The hypochondriac body – the organs have been destroyed and there is nothing that can be changed about it.
- The paranoid body – the organs are continually under attack by outside forces.
- The schizo body – wages its own internal struggle against its own organs.
- The drugged body – the body is ineffective and inefficient and should be changed.
- The masochist body – The organs must be flayed and pain must take place to reach their full potential. The 'wants' of each body without organs are not uniform and so cannot be compared well against one another. (Deleuze and Guattari 2013b, 174)

Much of this is put down to the process of the desiring-machine where Deleuze and Guattari oppose the traditional Freudian idea of the unconscious and instead propose that desire is a real productive force that people consciously seek. They went away from traditional Marxist thought by arguing that desire was not merely symbolic but was constructive, for example, machinic, and so produced desire as material reality. In capitalism, they discerned, however, that desire became destructive due to the repression by the state in which the desire was being carried out:

There are no desiring-machines that exist outside the social machines that they form on a large scale; and no social machines without the desiring machines that inhabit them on a small scale. (Deleuze and Guattari 2013a, 373)

Those in society whose 'desire' to be able to present as homosexual in public (e.g. rather than having to keep this identity hidden due to legal recourse), which, as Deleuze and Guattari explain, is positive in itself as a desire, becomes a destructive force. Because the homosexual is unable to escape from the heteronormative system of capitalism, they have to repress their homosexuality to 'appear normal', which can have harmful real-life effects:

The homophobic nature of society does make lesbians and gays more likely to develop some psychological problems, such as constant tension, self-hatred, and depression, which in turn lead to higher rates of suicide and alcohol and drug abuse among gays and lesbians than among straights. Running through these problems is the failure to achieve a harmonious integration of one's diverse identities. (Thio 2010, 253)

This can certainly be seen in the Furries, in that lifestylers indicated in their answer that they were suffering from more stress due to their perceived stigma just for 'being a Furry' than those who just saw their membership as a hobby. For Deleuze and Guattari, the masochist body can only be fulfilled through 'intensities of pain' (2013b, 176), and for the lifestylers, this is best done through the notion of 'attraction and repulsion':

Attraction and repulsion produce intense nervous states that fill up the body without organs to varying degrees … becoming a woman and many other things as well, following an endless circle of eternal return. (Deleuze and Guattari 2013a, 19)

For some Furries, their BwO is hard to define and is in constant struggle and pain especially when they have to explain their identity to others:

Furry: It's very hard to explain to someone what being a Furry is. And any time I have tried they always slightly misunderstand something (completely accidentally) and it can make it seem like something quite different very easily. The fact it's tough to understand what it is, (you basically have to live it to know what it's like), is likely what makes others struggle to understand/empathise with us.

For the masochist body compared to the other BwO modes, there is a risk that it will become what Deleuze and Guattari refer to as 'cancerous', as often the wants of the masochist body are not uniform, it can struggle to fit within the institution. This is where attraction and repulsion come into play, and thus the masochist body will 'resubmit it to its rule or restratify it, not only for its own survival, but also to make possible an escape from the organism, the fabrication of the "other" BwO on the plane of consistency' (2013b, 189). In the Furry Fandom (acting as an institution) it has been dictated to the Furry what is and is not acceptable for their identity. Their masochist body will, to avoid becoming cancerous, have to restratify itself into this Furry social order to be accepted by the institution, often with discomfort to the individual. For Deleuze and Guattari, the masochist body is far from ideal because it is seen as destructive, and in psychoanalytical terms is harmful to the person pursuing it.

Sadly, there are many lifestyler Furries who are not happy with their Furry identity. In this way they enact a masochist BwO which is harmful to their identity and psychological well-being:

> **Furry:** No one I know in real life knows I'm a furry. It would be social suicide for me to reveal it, so in an indirect way I guess I am stigmatized.
>
> **Furry:** I've been around people quite a few times insulting or making fun of the group who didn't know that I identify as a furry. It's sort of like it's the last thing it's still okay to make fun of.
>
> **Furry:** Talking to people who aren't in the fandom about the fandom ... there's always a layer of awkwardness in the conversation. The general public just doesn't know what the fandom is. There's no corporation or movie studio branding what being a 'Furry' means. There are entertaining parodies in today's media, but their viewers don't really know what's being exaggerated. How do you describe such a diverse fandom to someone outside the fandom when members of the fandom will debate what being a Furry means?

For Deleuze and Guattari, the schizo body is that which escapes the Oedipal, in that it resists the ascription of traits imposed on it by the familial 'I'll no longer say daddy-mommy – and he keeps his word' (2013b, 411). The schizo body is revolutionary as it goes in the other direction:

> That of microphysics, of molecules insofar as they no longer obey the statistical laws: waves and corpuscles, flows and partial objects that are no longer dependent upon the large numbers; infinitesimal lines of escape, instead of the perspectives of the large aggregates. (Deleuze and Guattari 2013a, 278)

The schizo body makes it possible for seemingly incompatible or perverse elements of an identity to coexist much like what can happen in highly identified Furries. These are constantly in conflict with the notion of their human body, for some they reject this body and see themselves as something not entirely human (Gerbasi et al. 2008).

As one of the first things ascribed to BwO is 'races, cultures and their Gods' (Deleuze and Guattari 2013a, 85); highly identified Furries construct their schizo body in direct opposition to this. Even those who do not identify themselves as 'not entirely' human and thus accept their species for what it is think about their identity in a very post-human and thus schizo bodied way.

For many respondents to the research, there was a very real awareness that often the body is ascribed traits that may not be complementary to the identity:

> Furry: It's helped me be more open with myself. It's helped me be more accepting of other people and the 'mask' that we all wear from day to day. I've learned to really look at people's personalities, not just their features and surface traits.

For a lot of respondents recognizing the 'mask' that they were supposed to wear in ordinary society as opposed to their Furry body was a big issue. The mask is important when it comes to faciality, with Deleuze and Guattari particularly conflating the schizo body with the rhizomatic processes of maintaining all the different faces that society makes people present; 'schizos lose their sense of the face, their own and others, their sense of landscape and the sense of language and its dominant significations all the time' (2013a, 219). They point out that multiple sub-identities or masks are able to coexist with the dominant identity that the person has to present. But this creates the Schizo BwO in those with marginalized identities who have to then struggle internally over which masks to show and which to keep hidden. The Furries understand that their fandom's values in cultural capital is not the same as 'real-life' institutions and this conflict is fought internally on their BwO. This is one of the prime reasons why some Furries fit the concept of BwO as set out by Deleuze and Guattari; lifestylers are rejecting the subjectivation of imposed social constructs via their identity construction. Many who suffer from stigmatization are presenting a schizo body because they are unable to relate their body to their environment. This is due to the systems (whether it be institutional or societal) that insinuate they are not 'allowed' to be that person. The schizo body is present in those who are in stigmatized groups, and once again it is why lifestylers are representative of the schizo body. Frosh states 'using psychosis as a metaphor for normal postmodern functioning produces a pessimistic reading' (1991, 133). However, for those who suffer from stigmatization due to this system, it is the only way that they *do* see it; lifestyler Furries have given pessimistic readings on how they view their identity and the stigmatization around it.

From research into sexual and gender minorities by Vicky M. Mays and Susan D. Cochran, those who are subjected to stigmatization due to their non-heteronormative sexuality or non-cis gender have an increased vulnerability to psychological comorbidities (2001). There have been several studies suggesting that the homosexual community suffers under the minority stress model (APA 2012) which states that, due to homophobia, gay men suffer greater physical and mental health problems than straight men (Williams et al. 2003). One of these stress factors that has been investigated by the IARP is the use of concealment strategies, where a Furry has concealed their identity as a Furry to avoid the negative stigma that may come with being part of that group. Concealment strategies have been found to be harmful among gay men concealing their HIV-positive status due to constant self-monitoring by the individual to stop themselves being exposed (Pachankis 2007). The IARP found that 'approximately 50% of Furries believe that their being Furry was not a choice' (Plante et al. 2015). In their research they set out to discover whether these groups adopted concealment strategies. They found that in many cases this affected the Furries' self-esteem (ibid.) and thus could put Furries using concealment strategies in the same group as those suffering under the minority stress model. In my research, I found that concealment strategies are relatively common within the Furry Fandom, which is consistent with the IARP findings.

However, a difference was found when it came to experiencing stigmatization in those who self-identified as Furries but did not have fursonas and Furries who considered themselves hobbyists in general. This in turn cemented my need in research to discuss my finding that stigmatization within the fandom changes by how heavily identified a Furry is. When I began the research, I hypothesized that Furries with no fursona (and so less of an identification with the fandom) would feel less stigmatized than highly identified Furries. My hypothesis ended up being correct when my data revealed that those with no fursona did feel less stigmatized both online and offline compared to Furries with one fursona or two or more fursonas. As well as this, Furries with two or more fursonas did not experience stigmatization as strongly as those with one fursona. This is because, as noted by the IARP, Furries use their fursonas as authenticating an 'idealized' self; I argue then that those with two or more fursonas do not feel the same levels of attachment to their fursonas as Furries who focus on having one fursona. Someone who has the ability to constantly change their design of fursona is obviously not experiencing a post-human connection with their fursonas in the way that lifestylers do.

Many try to conceal their status of being in a minority group and often these minorities will identify with other group members, usually for support. The IARP found 'that highly identified Furries are motivated to strongly identify with the Furry Fandom because the group affords members the psychological needs of belonging and intergroup distinctiveness' (Reysen et al. 2016, 641). This phenomenon, even though it seems counter-intuitive to want to identify with a group that you do not want others to know you are a part of, can produce positive effects. Having a group to fall back on is highly important for many minorities; studies have found that without this support network, they may experience negative effects due to social and emotional isolation (Grossman and Kerner 1998; McNicholas 2002). I expected to find that Furries who were open about being a Furry in the offline world would have experienced more stigmatization. This is because much of the general public only know what they have seen on television (Soh and Cantor 2015, 1) when asked about who and what Furries are.

But I was incorrect in this assumption, with respondents in my study stating that they were more likely to feel stigmatized in the online space, often mentioning harsh backlashes to their online Furry avatars. This may be because several of the respondents mentioned that they had felt a lot of stigmatization online by trolls and anti-Furry forums like r/Furryhate – this led to some even creating alternative accounts for Furry use and non-Furry use. Data results were at odds with my hypothesis, which presumed that there would be a much higher rate of stigmatization offline and much less online. This was due, in part, to other studies that have been conducted by the IARP showing more stigmatization offline. My research shows that Furries use specific sites to disclose their Furry identity. In keeping with much internet research which shows that people cultivate certain 'online personas' dependent on what site they are on. Long and Chen (2007) suggest that people often choose to disclose their identities in environments where they will receive a positive reaction. Many of the respondents in my research who said they did not feel stigmatized online had further clarified that this was due to non-disclosure; they were only disclosing their Furry status on Furry websites and using non-Furry avatars on other sites. This phenomenon of fearing stigmatization in the online rather than the offline space is not unique to the Furries but has also occurred in another fandom. In the research done at the Chicago Tardis Convention (*Doctor Who*), the researchers found that much fan activity was still taking place in person 'partly out of a fear, it seems, of being exposed to ridicule or mockery online' (Booth and Kelly 2013, 65).

There is also another distinct difference in my research, compared to the IARP. In that I have identified that there is intra-stigmatization between lifestylers and hobbyists. 'Drama' was often quoted in relation to those moaning about being stigmatized in response to the question, 'Is there anything you dislike about the Furry Fandom?':

Furry: There is plenty of 'Furry' drama that occurs in this fandom. Some people are extremely sensitive and look to bend words to start drama.

Furry: The people who use slang like 'Fursecution' and all that, also the drama that many try to cause.

Furry: Maybe we should try to learn to be better at handling drama or adversity from others inside of the group …

Going back to the research by Dank on homosexuality in which he states that a gay man 'knows that he is no queer, pervert, dirty old man, and so on' (1975,

224), echoes the way that many hobbyists place themselves cognitively in the community. For example, 'As I am not a Furry who (going from the stereotypes) is sexually deviant, interested in bestiality etc. then I am not like *those* Furries.' Following on, those who position themselves as a hobbyist, protect themselves from stigmatization because they perceive that it is not their version of 'Furry' that is being stigmatized. In the research data, Dank's theory was present in comments from fifty-one users, such as the following:

Furry: The weirdoes in it. I'm a very professional normal person, and I don't like being associated with the stranger side of the fandom. We aren't all dysfunctional basement dwellers. I hate people who make it their sole identity. It defines them and is their lifestyle.

Furry: So I am a Furry but sometimes I feel like I'm not like other Furries. Seeing people treat being a furry as a lifestyle rather than a hobby is rather stupid in my eyes, some people just take it too seriously or get into it too much. Other than that, it's a relatively cheery thing.

But this has the downside that hobbyists can sometimes alienate and sometimes vilify those who see being a Furry as a lifestyle and something that is part of their identity. A comment in my study, which was particularly interesting, highlighted this difference:

Furry: While it is a fantastic and liberating experience to be a part of, an important thing is to never forget 'Furry' is not a monolithic construct. We are as diverse as it gets and even more, seeing the openness to all manner of quirks. It is important to know what 'shard' of a fandom you belong to and stick with the like-minded. A thing that many tend to forget about. / And, by extension, to be aware of these sub-clusters when performing studies like these.

There have also been issues raised about criminal deviancy within the fandom concerning some of the more prominent Furries and attendees at conventions. In my research, I found that some Furries were concerned about 'popufurs' getting away with misguided and even criminal behaviour. This has been exacerbated by these kinds of activities at Furry conventions. One well-publicized event was RainFurrest, a convention that no longer runs. The hotel which had hosted the event since 2011 cancelled their contract with the Furries in 2015; this was due to 'multiple examples of flamboyant drunken and other inappropriate public behaviour from new teenage attendees, including severe vandalism' (Patten 2016). RainFurrest board members took partial responsibility for failing to hold attendees to 'standards of behaviour':

> We as a convention were entirely unwilling to hold people accountable to standards of behavior. Although we laid out policies to create a healthy and respectful space, we didn't enforce them. We didn't need to raise our standards in 2015; we needed to adhere to the standards we already claimed to have. More importantly, we needed to have been doing so consistently all along. Other cons have almost identical language regarding expected public dress and behavior in their codes of conduct, but they don't seem to have the problems we did with people using the headless lounge as a petting zoo or having to summon the ambulance multiple times per con for drug overdoses. We had become a 'safe' space to violate the rules, because we had a long history demonstrating that there would be no consequences. (WikiFur 2016)

The board member noted one of the problems that has been echoed by Furries in this book when it comes to criminal deviancy. As a result, because they were not able to constrain behaviour within the parameters deemed appropriate, they were forced to shut down. This example demonstrates that when an institution does not 'enforce' rules, it often fails.

For Furries, acceptance has meant that, as an institution, there is little discrimination towards those of different sexualities. However, the term 'hug-box' is commonly used to criticize this aspect of the Furry Fandom, which suggests that the community is based on unconditional tolerance to the point that it is detrimental as all opinions (including negative or harmful ones) are accepted. This general complaint that because the fandom was based on being open to everyone, sometimes Furries would ignore extreme behaviour that they should have regulated. There is also a debate among different Furries within the fandom as to whether sexuality should be important to a Furries' identity at all. The Furries are not alone in these arguments as the level of fan engagement is often argued between fans in other fandoms. It is often the question over 'authenticity', who is the real fan and who would be described as a 'fan boy'? (Locke 2012). 'Acceptance', in general, being a common trend in the Furry Fandom has been found in previous studies by the IARP. They found that nearly 80 per cent of Furries in their studies believe acceptance is 'a fundamental component of the community' (Reysen et al. 2015a, 42). An important finding in my word establishes and categorizes a social norm in the community and therefore it can be said that the Furry Fandom promotes tolerance and acceptance in their collective identity. But, these comments highlight that Furries sometimes feel that they should remember to 'stick with' other Furries who share their beliefs. Their comments also act as a warning to researchers to be mindful of this when researching. This opens up an interesting avenue for future research into how deep this division really is as I have only just started to investigate these in this book.

Conclusion

The aim of this chapter has been to analyse previous research by the IARP, which has predominantly labelled the Furry community as a whole as stigmatized. Studies by Roberts et al. (2015b) present Furries as a homogenous group who all feel stigmatization at the same level, but this is not the case. The main reason for this is that much of their data has been taken from fan conventions and Furry-dedicated websites. This means it is more likely that highly identified Furries will attend due to monetary reasons, and from websites that are aimed specifically at Furries, with those who see it as a hobby visiting on a less regular basis.

There is no doubt that Furries are a stigmatized group, as shown by reactions to them in the online space from trolls and the portrayals of them in the media such as 'Fur and Loathing in Las Vegas'. However, labelling all Furries as stigmatized at the same level is problematic as different levels of identification can affect the levels to which a fan can feel stigma: 'A strong sense of group identification can, in some ways, make people more vulnerable to stigmatization' (Major et al. 2003, 155). Lifestyler Furries perceive stigmatization against Furries as more damaging to their well-being than those who see it as a hobby. We also have to remember that the Furry Fandom members are mostly under the age of 25, and in my research I found most of my respondents to be 18–19 years old. But, there are many members of the fandom who are adolescents, which can create problems for stigmatization. There is some evidence to suggest that adolescents who were frequent users of social networking communities experience more psychological distress due to negative reinforcement as well (Hong et al. 2014; Sampasa-Kanyinga and Lewis 2015). This may be because some communities reinforce increased risk-taking (Long and Chen 2007; Ridout et al. 2012) or encourage users to cultivate an image of a 'perfect life' (Chou and Edge 2012; Radovic et al. 2017, 12). This means that younger members of the fandom could suffer more stigmatization simply because they are more susceptible to it because of their age.

I use Deleuze and Guattari to talk about highly identified Furries because their work notes how people with different identities are stigmatized because they represent 'non-meaning' or a different kind of 'body':

> This kind of group is thus involved in a perpetual struggle against any possible inscription of non-meaning: various roles are reified by a phallic appropriation along the model of the leader or of exclusion. One is part of such a group so as to collectively refuse to face up to nothingness that is, to the ultimate meaning of the projects in which we are engaged. (Guattari 2015, 78)

To explain further, Guattari theorized that there is no access to a 'true self' or identity because as soon as we are born, institutions and societal norms are immediately enforced upon us and that 'the individual can only speak in the context of the discourse of the Other' from that point on (ibid.). Guattari argued that signifiers changing is often for antipathetic or negative reasons: 'identification with the prevailing images of the group is by no means static, for the badge of membership often has links with narcissistic and death instincts that it is hard to define' (2015, 227). This has been seen within the Furry Fandom when it comes to the 'acceptability' of pornography consumption (to be discussed in the next chapter) and how far a Furry is allowed to 'identify' with their fursona. This split comes in the parts of the group that want to distance themselves from it so as not be stigmatized as mentally ill or deviant by the media or by trolls online.

However, the limitation with my research is that, as with other studies on stigmatization, 'when it is detected, devalued group members are often reticent to report that they have been victims of stigmatization' (Crocker et al. 1998). Some of the Furries in this study, although it was anonymously collected data, may feel that they did not want to report stigmatization as they did not want to reinforce negative stereotypes from outside society. Also, because many complained about others causing 'drama' they may have not want to be seen as 'causing drama' themselves.

We should not ignore, however, that there are a proportion of Furries who still feel significantly stigmatized. Online abuse is rife with specific Furry hate groups. It is unsurprising that data from this study concluded that many Furries now feel more stigmatized online than they do in the offline environment, the opposite of the hypothesis I began my research with. Many of the stories focused on anonymous abuse they would get for simply having a 'Furry'-looking avatar:

> Furry: I hadn't [been stigmatized] until I opened a twitter account for my art. I wanted to have a more personal space to 'reveal' the artist behind the art. Less than 20 posts to the account when I posted some questions and words of encouragement when FurAffinity's website went down. Within 24 hours someone without my consent stuck me into a Twitter 'list' (no idea what that is) that was labeled as 'animal rapists'. I'm a somewhat devout buddhist that will take the time to stop talking to move an earthworm off pavement or asphalt onto grass or dirt. It hurt to be thrown into the fray JUST because my twitter avatar was my fursona – an art piece I made myself, and just because I posted positive words on a furry associated twitter account. It also set off feelings and memories of my own childhood sexual assault that I had thought I moved past and gotten over. Since then I've made my twitter account a little more private but, I do try to market myself as an artist so I can't exactly lock everyone out.

Unfortunately for the Furry Fandom, whether an individual is highly identified or not, they are still being stigmatized for their interests. For lifestylers who are already unhappy with the prospect of being 100 per cent human (and thus the prospect of being post-human or Therian), this can have a detrimental effect on their self-esteem and thus their identity construction. Researchers should be aware in future research that, as with many other fandoms, Furries are subject to a geek hierarchy. This means that those at the bottom (hobbyists) will have different experiences when it comes to stigmatization which thus far had not been addressed.

6

Pornography in the Furry Fandom

To what extent are furries sexually motivated, and what explains any sexual motivation? Regarding the second question, we doubt that most people would find the prospect of behaving or dressing like an anthropomorphic animal to be sexually arousing. Assuming that some furries do experience sexual arousal in this context, the question remains why.

– Hsu and Bailey (2019)

Porn studies

People have a hard time talking about porn. But pornography has been generating revenues of between 12 and 14 billion US dollars per year since 2004 (Williams 2004, 2), and have remained at this level for over a decade (NBC News 2015); this is despite many people denying they have watched any in their entire lives. I will never have this polite luxury ever again now that I have publicly written a whole chapter on the subject where I acknowledge analysing thousands of images – one of the few people in the world who can at least use the excuse that I was consuming porn for 'research reasons'.

This reluctance to talk about pornography has meant that many fan communities have faced misconceptions when it comes to their pornography consumption by the general public, and this has been particularly prevalent in criticism of the Furry Fandom. This may perhaps be why researchers, who wish to help show to the world that the Furries are not 'deviants who fuck animals', have sometimes shied away from this subject not wanting to draw further attention to it – again, people have a hard time talking about porn. But this is why I made a point in researching and including a whole chapter on it in this book. Because, if we don't publicly and academically clear up these misconceptions, people will continue believing these false assumptions regarding the Furries, which I have highlighted in Chapter 5.

A Gallup survey in 2013 reported that 66 per cent of Americans believed that pornography is 'morally wrong' even though statistics prove that most of those 66 per cent may still be watching pornography despite publicly proclaiming it to be 'wrong' (Durham 2015, 1). So, we know people will lie to researchers, and possibly themselves, when it comes to pornography use. It is then expected that although pornography is viewed as morally wrong, Furry pornography, which is considered unusual and therefore abhorrent (for reasons I will outline throughout this chapter), is vastly misunderstood.

But what then, is Furry pornography? Furry pornography displays fursonas in erotic situations; if you were to replace the image you have in your mind of say a pornographic actress in a scene and swap it for a fursona, you would be – to use a popular phrase – on the money. Why the outrage then if it is just a simple swap? It is because for many outside the Furry Fandom and for those with no experience with pornography besides Page 3 girls and 'lads' mags', the fursona can be mistaken to represent a literal animal. As Laura Kipnis identifies, we get used to certain kinds of pornography and as Furry pornography is outside this map of what we understand to be pornography, we are liable to call it deviant (2006, 120). One major part of this is due to the hierarchy we seem to place on what is acceptable versus what's problematic, that is, what is pornographic and what can be considered erotic art, and as Joanna Russ argues,

> Well, let's just say to call something by one name when you like it and another when you don't is like those married ladies we all know who call what they do 'making love' while what is done by singles in bars is 'shallow and trivial sex', and what homosexuals do is 'perversion'. (There are also those folks who call a work of that supports the status quo 'art' and works that questions it 'political'.) (2014, 82)

One of the accusations that are levelled at the fandom is that all Furries are obsessed with pornography and that is the only reason the fandom exists. In the data available, however, this 'excess availability' has proven mostly unfounded. Most artwork submissions to popular Furry art sites such as Furaffinity.com and others labelled as 'mature' or 'adult' are in the vast minority of submissions with up to 90 per cent submissions each year being 'safe for work'.[1] What has helped from an academic perspective is that it has been very easy to see an adherence to labelling from the Furry Fandom for a long time period, which has made it easier to collect this data and make a comparison. This is in part due to the fact that Furry Fandom fan fiction and its related images have been heavily self-regulated since the early 1990s (Gold 2015, 29). Kyell Gold has argued that this strict self-regulation has come from Furries trying to avoid the association with erotic material to the point where one semi-erotic scene in a Furry fiction would immediately be categorized as mature/adult compared to other fandoms where similar scenes would be considered innocuous enough to be sold under general rather than erotic categories (ibid.). Furries also made a huge effort to restrict sales of these materials to minors despite not being required under legal legislation as a way to try to detract from the anti-pornography brigades' cries of 'won't somebody think of the children?!' This enforcement of material by the Furries is above and beyond what they need to do legally as fan fiction is very rarely regulated when it comes to erotic material; it was only in 2010 where Japan placed a ban on erotica sales to minors, for example:

> The Non-existent Crimes Bill. The bill regulates the sale and renting of 'harmful publications' to Japanese youth: material that is 'sexually stimulating, encourages cruelty, and/or may compel suicide or criminal behaviour' in people under the age of 18. (Leavitt and Horbinski 2012)

Another factor of anti-pornography arguments lead with the 'assumption that pornography express[es] the power and the pleasure of heterosexual men', but this argument is unconvincing when it comes to non-heteronormative pornography and indeed fantasy-like pornography using fursonas. In Furry pornography, who is being objectified? Is it possible to objectify a fursona? If we believe it is an animal, then can we advance the category of 'man and woman' on these made-up entities?

As I noted in my methodology section in the introduction chapter of this book, I have used analytic memos to analyse Furry pornography. The paradigms that were chosen are specifically those which deal with 'fantasy' pornography and pornography from the anime fandom. This is because the anime fandom has been found to share certain visual aesthetics with the Furry Fandom and share similar demographics in the research by the IARP (Plante et al. 2016, 5).

My work also acknowledges and follows the paradigm shift in pornography studies, as described by Fiona Attwood:

> Work that has emerged from the paradigm shift has, in one way or another, marked the development of attempts to contextualize pornographies – in relation to other media genres, aesthetics and hierarchies of cultural value, in relation to a variety of consumer groups and in relation to the broader frameworks of cultural regulation and the lives of their producers and consumers. The value of this approach is that pornographies are conceptualized in line with theoretical accounts of cultural and sexual construction, discussed in terms of their social and political significance, and investigated with methodologies that have been shown to be appropriate for research that deals with issues of media production, representation and consumption. (2011, 14)

The use of analytic memos with which to research pornography is therefore appropriate. As Saldana notes,

> Just as no two people most likely interpret a passage of text the same way, no two people will most likely interpret a visual image the same way. Each of us brings our background experiences, values system, and disciplinary expertise to the processing of the visual, and thus our personal reactions, reflections, and refractions. Spencer (2011) advocates that readings of the visual should adopt a sociological lens with a critical filter through 'thick description' analytical narratives. (2016, 60)

By situating the use of Furry pornography within the cultural aspects of the Furry Fandom, this avoids previous work which has situated all kinds of pornography together without contextualizing the consumption in the culture or subculture in which it has appeared. This will situate this work in the new paradigm rather than viewing this pornography consumption as part of a tenacious 'media effects' theory that has been used in the past (Attwood 2014, 1191).

There has been some recent interest in Furry pornography and sexual habits with Hsu and Bailey (2019) researching male Furries and subsequently diagnosed them with autoanthropomorphozoophilia.[2] A response to this paper was given by B. Terrance Grey (2020) in which they believed that a 'conditioned fetish' was more appropriate to 'explain' Furry pornography/ sexuality. To me, these seem like a similar kind of pathologizing that has been common in fan studies and so I wanted to analyse both the images as well as data from Furries.

Finally, it became important to me to investigate Furry pornography because it opens up questions about our assumption of power and representation in fantasy pornography. Counter-intuitively, however, I am not about to tell you that Furry pornography has been able to escape these shackles. I found that although Furry pornography is complete fantasy and that Furries could potentially draw their fursona in any fantasy scenario, Furry pornography seems to adhere and reinforce many cultural norms we already have about 'regular' human pornography. This does not make it any less noteworthy, perhaps more so, because if we could draw a fursona doing anything, why do we revert back to a pornography 'comfort zone'? I intend to answer this question throughout this chapter.

Analysis of Furry pornography

Art style

The first and most obvious aspect of Furry pornography is that it is drawn in a cartoon or animal style which is why the IARP have often likened Furries to the anime fandom (which uses similar aesthetics). In Japan, the attitude to animated pornography has been remarkably different to those in the western hemisphere and animated pornography has been described as not only flourishing but also constituting 'a large and significant genre' in anime (Shamoon 2004, 78). Deborah Shamoon's research has found that different anime genres cater for many different sexual preferences while some genres such as yaoi and shoji manga overlap, with many readers enjoying both homosexual and heterosexual stories (ibid., 86).[3] Undoubtedly, there are many people in Japan and around the world who enjoy these genres despite many critics of pornography (who are not just anti in total) decrying any pornography which doesn't depict 'real sex'.[4] This is, predictably, just sex scenes between a married man and woman, and cartoon pornography, and certainly Furry and anime pornography, falls under this criticism of not 'real sex' due to the fact that it is drawn.

It has often been noticed that these critics use a false concern about health when it comes to pornography, with John Ellis noting that 'the metaphors of "health" hovers over ... healthy sexuality is a sexuality which is functional within a relationship' (1992, 150). But why should a healthy sexuality just be functional in what is presumably a heterosexual relationship to boot? I am in agreement with Shamoon who argues that cartoon pornography is popular for the very reason that it is *not* 'real sex' because it can show relationships which are not part of a heterocentric society and that parts of sex that are hidden in traditional pornography can be exposed. Scott McCloud notes:

> when you look at a photo or a realistic drawing of a face, you see it as the face of another. But when you enter the world of cartoon you see yourself ... the cartoon is a vacuum into which our identity and awareness are pulled, an empty shell that we inhabit which enables us to travel in another realm. We don't just observe cartoon, we become it. (1993, 84)

Essentially, traditional pornography can be very boring for some, and I am inclined to extrapolate from McCloud's logic that it is much easier for someone to place themselves as the cartoon rather than onto a human face, which can make consuming cartoon pornography far more pleasurable. As well as this, human pornography is incredibly limited to what can actually happen, whereas the benefit of cartoon pornography is that 'only the imagination of the artist can limit the action' (Shamoon 2004, 87). Bruce LaBruce (famous queer artist and pornography director) has certainly lamented this before:

> I must confess that I always lose interest in the explicit scenes when I'm shooting a porno. I guess that probably isn't a good sign. The mechanics of porn really aren't very sexy at all, and it's very difficult to shoot sex in a novel way, so it always seems like the same thing every time you do it. (McGlotten 2014, 372)

This problem, however, does not ever limit cartoon pornography. They can show instances that are often hidden in human pornography such as the view of penetration and ejaculation from inside the vagina or anus. They can even achieve feats that are physically impossible to produce in human actors due to the intense amount of damage or pain that could be produced such as a penis penetrating through the cervix. This could provide release to those who have an interest in seeing those feats but would rather not destroy the body of another. And I noted several of these instances in my analytic memos, including this one of a male and female fox fursona scene:

> This piece utilises a feature of fantasy pornography that Shamoon mentioned, in that is it possible to draw the act of ejaculation occurring within the vagina. This piece is filled with hyper-realism with the over-exaggerated sized penis and breasts.

Laura Mulvey has argued that cinema often portrays 'a hermetically sealed world which unwinds magically, indifferent to the presence of the audience, producing for them a sense of separation and playing on their voyeuristic phantasy' (1992, 25); it is the same for cartoon pornography, it allows viewers to put themselves in the fantasy, any fantasy if they choose to.

But it can be strange for others to consider the legitimacy of Furry pornography as something that provides sexual pleasure due to the fact that when it comes to pornography and erotic art, there are 'classifications of those who view the images: they are social, cultural and moral designations of people as well as objects' (Nead 1993, 145). Form is notoriously difficult to 'get right' when it comes to animals; Deleuze and Guattari were incredibly suspicious of form when it came to becoming-animal. A solution was not provided in *A Thousand Plateaus* but rather in Deleuze's book on the work of artist Francis Bacon. This is where Deleuze suggested that 'painting has to extract the Figure from the figurative' (2003, 8) with 'isolating the Figure [will] be the primary requirement. The figurative (representation) implies the relationship of an image to an object that it is supposed to illustrate' (ibid., 2), hence moving from the figure to the figural. Deleuze is suspicious of form, because in his discussion about photographs 'it is not a figuration of what one sees, it is what modern man sees' (ibid., 11) with so much art being seen through a culture-laden lens of the viewer. And this is the problem with pornography, but by using animals to represent their sexual desires in their pornography, Furries are taking sensibilities about the human form out of the equation and although that works for some, others find it abhorrent as 'we should only use the human form for gratification and sexual signification'. These people often forget that we have been using the animal form without any question of morals in our art for century. Postmodern artist John Issacs notes that the animal is perfect for our projects when it comes to how to include ourselves in the pieces:

> So this is where the animal works, for me. It has this ability to be the viewer, for the viewer to project into it. ... Identity is something that I don't want for something like this, I don't want it to be a man with a moustache, or glasses, or no hair, I want it to be the person who's looking at it. So it has to be without an identity. (Baker 2000, 76)

This is why I suggest that the art style that the Furries choose to engage with in the creation of their pornography (and general fursonas and artwork) should be seen as 'without' identity. The use of cartoon to present their pornography allows the consumer to not imitate the animal (and therefore suggest a sexual attraction to animals themselves) but to incorporate the signification of ferality. This is because ferality in the bedroom is associated with sexual desire and is not representative of an actual animal. By using a cartoon art style, Furries can demonstrate any desire in their 'fantasy' pornography without getting bored or frustrated as we sometimes do with physically limited human pornography.

For Jenkins, slash and erotic fiction are used to 'stretch to accommodate a range of desires' (1992, 156) which is certainly what cartoon pornography is capable of doing. Speaking of the *poaching* we do from media texts, Jenkins suggests that erotic fan fiction authors can create 'an alternative sphere of cultural experience that restores the excitement and freedom that must be repressed to function in ordinary life' (2006, 42). This may be why there is plenty of transgender Furry pornography available.[5] By 'poaching' animals from their place in the animal kingdom, Furries create an alternative idea of the animal, which they use in both pornographic and non-pornographic practices, and this is particularly shown in the form of the animals which are used.

Form

This aspect of pornography has been one of the main sites of philosophical and ethical issues where anti-pornography critics (often feminists) have battled.

Feminists in particular have tended to be anti-pornography arguing that it is the female form which was being objectified by the male gaze. However, today (due to the further availability of genres other than heterocentric porn) this has become a rather reductive objection as it's argued that homosexual and transgender pornography do not have this bias (Williams 2004, 11). That is not to say we should not be looking for objectification still as often pornography can easily reveal power relations as Zabet Patterson notes:

> The habits of looking at internet pornography are as constitutive of the viewing experience as the images themselves, but, likewise, that these habits of looking insistently participate in inscribing power relations and social relations directly onto the body of the subject through gesture and repetition. (2004, 108)

I found that there are specific power relations in Furry artwork, some of which were highly visible. The IARP have consistently found that certain species are more popular as fursonas than others and that *canidae* were the most popular (Gerbasi et al. 2008).[6] This trend also transfers over to pornography as well with most pornography scenes featuring canines first and felines as a relatively distant second, with all other species becoming a distinct minority. Historically, Furries have given meaning to form in the species that have now become coded; a wolf is seen as sexually aggressive and foxes are considered submissive (Howl 2015, 52).

Furry pornography also implies social and power relations when it comes to beauty standards – it seems that even animated pornography cannot escape certain mindsets. But for Ellis, this is predictable because he argues that 'objects prone to fetishization are those which are already sexualised: underwear, visible parts of the body, the sound of clothes rustling, the smell of sweat' (1992, 163). And all of these make a very familiar appearance in Furry pornography from that which we see in human pornography especially when it comes to posing. Many fursonas wear erotic lingerie, have drawn sweat and sexual emissions, many have emphasis of showing eroticized parts of the body (if the fursona is not naked) such as protruding lumps in trousers or skimpy tops to enunciate breast shape and size. What is interesting to note, however, is that it becomes immediately obvious that what is being highlighted or eroticized is reflective of contemporary fashion. Kipnis notes that 'neither the culture nor the individual have had their particular borders for very long. These aren't timeless universals … all the motifs that obsess pornography – shift from culture to culture and throughout history' (2006, 122); and pornography has cultural and aesthetic style which changes over time – this is most prevalent in changes concerning body hair placement where we have seen pornographic images from the 1970s where everyone had pubic hair to today where body hair has been banished from most genres. Furry pornography has not been immune to this change of fashion, and Furry pornography follows many popular pornography motifs; although they are furry all over there is a lack of hair to function/act as pubic hair. Also, acceptability of bondage displays which used to be on the edges of traditional genres is commonly found and not deemed as strange, and perhaps most telling are provocative outfits such as lingerie and 'school-girl' outfits, which are very common as I noted in this memo:

> This female presenting fursona is doing a typical 'Boudoir' pose, often found in pornographic magazines, reminds me a lot of Playboy. All the clothing reminds me of what Ellis said in that we turned on by objects which are familiar to us and lingerie is definitely covered under this assumption. Maybe this is why many Furry Pornography stills include it?

The 'animals' in Furry pornography are seemingly adhering to cultural norms of human pornography (such as the lack of obvious pubic hair). Although this may be surprising to some, it should have been anticipated when reading theory from Adams's work, *Neither Man nor Beast: Feminism and the Defence of Animals*. As we know, most criticism of pornography is that it caters to the male gaze; heterosexual Furry pornography is certainly not immune to this and Adams notes that there is a historical alliance of sexual exploitation of both woman and animals:

> Empirical connections [that] reveal the intersection of the abuse of animals and the abuse of women expose another layer of intentional infliction of suffering by violent men, another way of comprehending the phenomenology of sexual violation. (2015, 146)

Adams notes in her work concerning abortion that women are often considered to have no moral agency over their bodies in contemporary debates and links this in the way that animals are also considered to have no moral agency; it is up to humans to decide 'what is best for them' (ibid., 55). Carlson also makes this connection:

> We consider Woman to occupy the same position as Animal, both being categories that serve to define Man by opposition … an embodied critique of the ways in which women are coerced into adhering to an impossible standard of beauty. (2011, 198)

This has also been noted in pornography in the representation of Black female performers, for example, who are equated with animals and thus insinuated to have less moral agency over their bodies than their white counterparts (Adams 1995; 2015, 153). We see this negative kind of connotation and that the incorporation of animal and human in pornography highlights this – when looking at representations of genitalia – and thus what they 'should' look like to be desirable. It is very important to note here that genitalia in Furry pornography tends to be similar in depiction to human anatomical parts rather than scientifically represented animal sexual organ. This is a key consideration because it shows that artists are following human beauty standards and represents yet another point as to why I confidently state that Furries are not engaging in a modified form of bestiality. If we examine female fursonas, they commonly have enlarged human breasts akin to porn stars rather than representations of animal mammary glands, and penises are rarely anything other than an extra-large porn star size. This was again something that I wrote in many of my analytic memos:

> This piece is intriguing as this is the first image from this random selection that has been most representative of the actual species it is trying to depict. It is clearly a fox due to its pointed ears, long tail and colouring (red and white). However, it is still subscribing to all common beauty (and porn) standards; it has human breasts and not mammary glands, a coy smile and is holding its breasts with hands instead of paws.

I follow the logic of Monique Wittig for why this may be as she argues that 'we have been compelled in our bodies and in our minds to correspond, feature by feature, with the *idea* of nature that has been established for us' (2006, 158; emphasis in original). Further, she suggests that often 'people understand the world according to how their physical bodies engage with/in the world' (ibid., 95). Therefore, a Furry drawing is presented as these 'traditional' porn forms because of the social cues that the Furries encounter in real life and in pornography, cues described by Butler in *Gender Trouble* (1990) and *Bodies That Matter* (1993). In human pornography massive breasts and huge penises are common in different subgenres, and many of the seductive poses common in Furry erotica are indicative of common human poses for pornographic magazines.

As well as this, the Furry Fandom being predominantly male means there is an insidious patriarchal reason why these kinds of genitalia are preferred in Furry pornography. Meredith Jones argues that 'the vulva and the vagina are sites of high anxiety in hetero-dominant patriarchies' (2017, 31); and you are hard-pressed to find a female fursonas who does not have what these cultures would describe as 'perfect'. Although Jones was discussing post-labiaplasty vulvas in her discussion on screen images, her views can be related to how fursonas' vulvas have been minimized:

> A post-labiaplasty vulva is one that has been positioned, visually and viscerally while its participation has been minimalized because its multiple folds have been whittled away leaving a single, accessible plane that simplifies its mode of being and diminishes its capacities. (Ibid, 32)

I cannot minimize the accusation that Furry pornography could often be construed as sexist as common representations would sometimes support that finding when it comes to the cultural referents of Furry genitalia. But as previously stated, I defend the Furry Fandom from accusations of bestiality quite staunchly; my research has highlighted an almost exclusive use of human genitalia in Furry pornography, a symbolic symbiosis between human and animal rather than trying to present a sexually attractive animal. This may be why some Furry pornography seems to recreate sexist human attitudes because the human elements of the fursonas are modelled on human pornography and patriarchal attitudes to how our sexual organs should look.

In Deleuze's analysis on the work of Francis Bacon, he noted that when a human head is replaced in artwork in favour for an animal head, 'it is not the animal as a form, but rather the animal as a trait' (2003, 21) and this is the form that occurs in Furry pornography; they are not portraying a literal animal in the pornography, only its feral traits. There is no doubt that these pictures are meant to excite sexually, but Furry pornography is laden with meaning as 'a body is not defined by the form that determines it nor as a determinate substance or subject … a body is defined only by a longitude and latitude' (Deleuze and Guattari 2013a, 260). Much like in the work of Bacon, the pornographic persona constitutes a *'zone of indiscernibility or undecidability between man and animal. Man becomes animal, but not without the animal becoming spirit at the same time, the spirit of man, the physical spirit of man'* (Deleuze 2003, 21; emphasis in original).

This is evident in as much as most fursonas (in general artwork as well as the pornography) are mostly shown as bipedal rather than representing how the literal species live (which is often with four feet on the ground). And this physicality also lends itself for rich analysis.

Depictions of sex and sexuality

As seen in discussions in this chapter surrounding form, there are major similarities with human sex seen in Furry pornography as opposed to animal sex. Many of the sexual acts that occur in Furry pornography are commonly seen in human pornography. It is easy to find images of 'doggy-style' sex including where one participant holds back the hands/arms of one participant while penetrating from behind, which is not an occurrence in the animal kingdom due to physiological differences. That is not to say that animals only engage in one sexual position – Bonobo monkeys are known to engage in missionary position and even fellatio (Hird 2009, 349). But importantly, many of the sexual acts depicted in Furry pornography are framed in a way that is only possible with the dexterity of a human-like bipedal anatomy and human-like thumbs for grip. Research into how animals have sex has been limited due to researchers focusing on a 'traditional evolutionary paradigm [with a] focus on reproduction' (ibid.). In this way, activities such as masturbation and oral sex have largely been ignored by animal behaviourists with books only beginning to address this in the last decade, with *Animal Homosexuality: A Biological Perspective* (Poiani 2010) arriving as one of the seminal texts in this field. Transspecies sex has also largely been considered impossible or ignored even though it does indeed occur in the animal kingdom (Nead 1993, 350). Research rarely investigates whether animals enjoy having sex – this may be why some view Furry pornography as abhorrent; they confuse the fursonas with real animals, and as animals are only here for our dominion over them and (of course) have sex only for the continuation of the species, they should not be perceived as having sexual agency. This attitude essentially follows the Evangelical Christian-Right line of thinking that some humans place on other humans in heterocentric society and this also translates over to animals.

And this suppression of any sexuality other than heterosexual has led to many hiding their true sexual feelings with no way of release and this is a factor to why Furry pornography is very effective for giving some people a sexual but also societal release. In studies by the IARP, a Furries fursona is seen as performing two major functions when it comes to identity formation: social identity and representation of possible selves (Roberts et al. 2015b, 45). This also extends itself to being a conduit for sexual and gender identity also. In the same work it is stated that '20 percent of Furries report having a fursona that is a different gender than their non fursonas self' and that 'the average Furry's fursonas is more likely to be bisexual than they are' (ibid., 46). This means that some Furries can then use Furry pornography to engage in a sexuality or experience a gender that they do not, or perhaps cannot, live in real life. For Noreen Giffney, writing about new queer cartoons, she states:

> Anthropomorphism, a staple of the animated feature, is again employed with new queer cartoons but is turned in on itself so that the analogy of humans becomes a critical lens through which societal norms are exposed to scrutiny and with the potential for change. (2009, 368)

Furry pornography and indeed other fantasy pornography also provide this function. My work entirely agrees with Giffney here when she asserts that 'the cartoon as a cultural product is often used to indoctrinate children and re-institute adults in the (correct) ways of heteronormativity' (ibid.).[7] By co-opting the cartoon which Giffney believes is used to indoctrinate into heteronormativity, Furries are instead using it as a form of resistance, a way to address sexuality they cannot express in real life due to societal pressure.

Furries are more likely to identify themselves as transgender compared to other fandoms (Plante et al. 2016, 11) and this may also be a reason why there is also a plethora of gender-bending found in Furry pornography. Ferreday found that cervine characters in particular are given symbolic transgender meaning in that they 'often display transgender characteristics as well as having the ability to shift species' (2011, 221). Furries are just as likely to be homosexual as they are bisexual or heterosexual as well as transgender. This means that queer erotica is seen as normal and acceptable in this fandom, compared to others where it may sit on the periphery. Within the fandom itself, 'sex and sexuality are simply not taboo topics' (Howl 2015, 49), which would suggest that sexuality in the Furry Fandom is considered as more acceptable on the whole, whether it is heteronormative or not.

Furry pornography tends to ignore limitations concerning interspecies relations as well as non-heteronormative relations. It is common to see pornographic images with two different species of fursonas engaging in sexual activity; it is also common to see pornographic images with different genders engaging in sexual activity. The arguments that these pictures constitute bestiality and that those who find them sexually exciting want to have sex with animals is a less-than convincing argument when you analyse the form. In their composition, they have more commonalities with form in human pornography than with real-life animal sex. These images represent human and animal hybridity and represent possible sexual desires of the consumer, not literal bestiality.

Furry porn as post-human?

I have made much of the fact in this book that lifestyler Furries are engaging with an identity that cannot be enacted in real life and their pornography utilizes this aspect as well in terms of post-humanism. Even hobbyist Furries who engage with the pornography can be considered in this framework as well. When I use this term, I think of the description used by Kim Toffoletti to visualize the post-human:

It is at the site of collapse between reality and fiction, referent and image, that
I locate the posthuman as a figuration that reformulates identity as a process of
transformation (2007, 17).

And I assert that this is also the way we can describe Furry identity and
pornography in that they enact this fantasy identity through the fusing together
of both human and animal. The sexuality that is shown in Furry pornography
(although I state should not be considered bestiality) is still not entirely human,
which is why it has been labelled unnatural and deviant (Soh and Cantor
2015). But Furry pornography can obtain new insights into the post-human
identity and I argue here that it has implications for Haraway's cyborg and
also her companion animal theories. And the first and foremost way it does
this is by Furry pornographies' displacing of the human as the entire object of
desire, by choosing to sexualize a human-nonhuman hybrid. Consequently,
the Furries are disregarding the humanist hierarchy which always put humans
firmly at the top and a system which philosophers (myself included) have long
lamented. In this way Furries are gaining gratification from replacing parts
of the human in their pornography and therefore they have 'replaced actual
human bodies in the public imagination' by making the human body obsolete
in their pornography (Springer 1996, 40). For MacCormack, 'the posthuman
is a direct challenge, not to the former human, but what it means corporeally
and discursively to be, or more correctly to count as human' (2009, 112). This
strengthens my assertion that Furry pornography is post-human; although it
replaces the human as the object of desire, it does not create a binary between
human and animal, instead fusing them together. I further use MacCormack
to strengthen my position:

> Collapse binary mechanisms which create human in opposition to non-human,
> living entity against inorganic matter and life against death. As humans and
> society become increasingly technological and virtual, is life itself able to be
> understood independent of the apparatuses and concepts which bring it to be
> and extend it, and through which it is negotiated? (Ibid.)

The 'negotiation' in Furry pornography is not only the body but also social
values of society. Although, I argue that Furry pornography can be seen to
enforce social norms (such as beauty aesthetics), it challenges them with an

emphasis on non-heteronormative couples and by using the symbolism of ferality. This is where Furry pornography can be related back to Haraway's cyborg in which she states that 'biology has intrinsically been a branch of political discourse, not a compendium of objective truth' (1991, 98); it does not matter that these pornographic images cannot be enacted in real life (as I have noted, there are specific problems in arguing for 'real sex' in pornography) as these images are more important in their political/societal symbolism. To go back now and try to answer MacCormack's question on negotiation, then, fantasy pornography and indeed Furry pornography cannot be understood independently from the society from which it has emerged. Fantasy pornography is often such because the desires within it are seen as deviant or 'impossible and not real sex' and the Furries use their pornography to exhibit an identity or sexuality that is stigmatized in real-world society. Although we would like to think of ourselves as becoming more tolerant, many microcosms within the UK and United States (where there are large Furry communities) do not accept non-heterosexual sexualities and refuse to understand transsexuality. Furry pornography can be a safe space online where these fluid and modern ideas of sex and sexuality can be experimented with away from these societies.

We also have to be aware of Furries' relationships with animals from a 'Western' society perspective as well, and this is where Furry pornography has implications for companion species theory. When Haraway moved away from the cyborg and onto the notion of companion species, she surmised that 'trans-species encounter value is about relationships among a motley array of living beings, in which commerce and consciousness, evolution and bioengineering, and ethics and utilities are all in play' (2003, 46). Additionally, as I explained in Chapter 4, it is unsurprising that the Furry Fandom commonly use canines as Haraway argues that 'they are not a projection, nor the realization of an intention, nor the telos of anything. They are dogs; i.e. species in obligatory, constitutive, historical, protean relationship with human beings' (ibid., 12). But this is why in a sense that dogs are seemingly perfect for a stigmatized community and why Furries are essentially combining the cyborg and companion species to produce a post-human identity in pornography. What should also be emphasized here is that enacting an identity online, which you may not be able to inhabit offline, is not new and once again makes me believe that Furries are being unfairly stigmatized when it comes to their pornography.

Many individuals find social and emotional support online when it comes to their sexual orientation (Coon Sells 2013, 894). Today, there are a plethora of websites and community support groups who can help an individual 'come out' if they so choose, but this is more challenging for Furries, as they are choosing a post-human identity and so there is little support outside the Furry Fandom community when it comes to this sexuality and sexual desire. As Furry pornography is exhibiting both human and animal traits, Furries are consequently creating a machinic heterogenesis in that their pornography transgresses species as well as that of nature and science.[8] Furry pornography is able to escape traditional views and inhibitions on sex without requiring a Furry to act on these desires. This is because the fursona which is used is not a real body and it is not a projection of a literal animal body either.

It is then important to keep in mind that unlike Robin Morgan's declaration that 'pornography is the theory, rape is the practice', Furry pornography cannot be carried out in real life and thus is post-human because it is 'without an image' (Williams 2004, 12). Therefore, this potentially makes Furry pornography more ethical than human pornography (it's drawn so what is the harm?). I have also noted that Furry pornography still upholds some societal 'rules' about what they find to be 'acceptable'. These ideas have permeated the fandom when what inner fandom reaction is to what they consider to be extreme genres, which we will discuss now.

Although I have noted that sex and sexuality are more openly acceptable as topics with the Furry Fandom, an ethical quandary has occurred for members within the fandom and even myself, for one genre in particular. Cub furs are a controversial part of the Furry Fandom as these are typically fursonas or fursuits that depict a newborn/infant version of the animal species that are being portrayed. Although many portrayals of baby Furries are usually benign and often meant to be cute, there are some who draw baby or cub fursonas in sexually explicit scenarios. This can cause issues for some as they view baby furs as being underage and so associate a sexually explicit Baby Fur/Cub Fur artwork as being paedophilic in nature. And for some hobbyists, having a sexual part of the fandom in the first place is not 'what they are here for':

Furry: I dislike how widespread the extreme fetishes seem to be. I do not
            want to see the very extreme fetishes such as scat, vore, whenever
            I am trying to look at normal furry art and stories.

Furry: I hate the amount of people who drag sex into a conversation that's
            not about sex. I really hate when people drag sex into a completely
            inappropriate setting. This happens with the Kink/fetish community
            sometimes too but not nearly as often as it happens with the furry
            community. What's worse though is how young the ages can be in
            the furry fandom - little kids really shouldn't be seeing or reading
            some of this stuff.

What we have to remember is that although the legal status of computer-
generated pornography varies around the world, many Western countries
(where the majority of the Furry Fandom is based) have strict laws regarding
these types of scenes. In the UK, both computer-generated and cartoon
drawings of children (or characters depicted as being under 18) are subject
to criminalisation if used in erotic or pornographic material (Durham 2015,
18). The strictest of these laws have led to multiple prosecutions including this
interesting case in Scotland:

> In February 2001, a Renfrewshire social worker was charged with possession
> of pornographic pictures made up of photographs of children's faces cut from
> magazines and pasted on to pornographic images downloaded from the internet.
> (Taylor and Quayle 2003, 21)

The reason a case such as this is so curious is because it does against the
traditional definition of child pornography when it comes to specific harm to
a specific child: 'To produce it, someone has to assault a child, or pose a child
in a sexualised way, and to make a photographic record of it' (ibid., 21). As
some have pointed out over the years, computer-generated or 'pseudo-child
pornography', as it is sometimes termed legally, has no real human child harmed
(ibid., 38). The rationale for equating cub fur to child pornography, however,
is still that the representation made in the drawing is a fursona which is meant
to be underage. In the UK, child pornography is covered by the Protection of
Children Act 1978 and pseudo-child pornography was updated in the Sexual
Offences Act 2003. In Section 7 of updated Protection of Children Act, a child
was defined in pseudo-pornography as the following:

> If the 'impression conveyed by a pseudo-photograph is that the person shown is
> a child' then it shall be treated for the purpose of the offence as showing a child.
> This is so where the predominant impression is to this effect notwithstanding
> some of the characteristics shown are those of an adult (s.7(8) of the PCA).

As the law specifies, 'person' cub fur is currently legally allowable in the UK,
and fursonas, as has been argued, are not people or literal animals. However,
some members of the Furry Fandom still define it this way, although it is not
enshrined in law:

> Furry: I do not like the fact that child pornography depicting furries is legal on
> some websites. I do not use web sites or support artists that allow 'cub porn'.
> I would prefer it if the community would shun/ excommunicate this part of the
> fandom, I would not advise bringing the community to a common knowledge
> level in the media until they are eliminated.

And this is why I must go back to post-humanism here to explain why
I argue that despite being legal, I agree with some Furries in that I do not
believe that Cub Fur can be considered ethical pornographic viewing. Maher
has argued that speciesism has meant that animals have not been granted
fair legal status. He argues that using the word person or personhood in legal
rulings has reinforced 'speciesist chains through an artificial science-based
relocation of a speciesist legal ontology by expanding the class of subjects in
relation to the human' (2014, 36). This has also been noted by Carey Wolfe
in as much as 'the language in which bioethics is discussed revolves around
largely quasi-legal notions such as consent, competence, rights to refuse'
(2010, 54). As such, I decided that as I have looked at Furry pornography
through a post-human lens, I cannot just ignore that a post-human legal
ethic exists, which states to get rid of the speciesist hierarchy. It would be
very easy for me to state, 'well if the law doesn't say cub fur is illegal then
it's fine', especially as I have found myself very sympathetic to this already
stigmatized community and did not want to contribute anything that could
make their suffering worse. However, I must follow my fellow post-humanist
philosophers in that

> an anthropomorphic ethic would attempt to bring the nonhuman up to a level
> of the human – equality feminism, animal rights based on how animals are 'like

us', the validation in all politics of similarity over difference and reification over transformation. (MacCormack 2009, 117)

To argue that animals are 'like us' means that animals represented as underage in cub fur pornography should be considered pseudo-child pornography. Especially because the Furry in question is becoming sexually gratified *because* the fursona depicted is underage. Wolfe argues that this way of thinking would be supported by Bentham's contention that, when it comes to ethical consideration for animals, it is about suffering rather than consciousness (cited in Wolfe 2010, 81). As pseudo-pornography of children is considered illegal, I argue the same rights apply for child fursonas using post-human bioethics.[9]

In a study by Tim Tate, it was suggested that just consuming child pornography produces a reinforcing effect that could well be applicable to computer-generated child pornography as well:

All paedophiles need to reassure themselves that what they are doing or want to do is OK. It [child pornography] validates their feelings, lowers their inhibitions and makes them feel that their behaviour is pretty normal in the context of this pornography they see other people doing it in the videos or the magazines and it reassures them. (1990, 24)

However, it should be noted that Tate's study seems to endorse a media effects theory which is criticized by Attwood (2014, 1191). This is because it seemingly ignored much research which has 'concluded that there was no connection between pornographic consumption and either change in sexual practices or an increase in sexual violence' (Segal 1993, 9). As mentioned by Lynne Segal, despite 'repeated exposure to slides showing highly "deviant" sexual activity, subjects showed no tendency to copy such practices' (ibid.). We can never be sure of the effects of viewing pornography such as cub fur has on the consumer because they are not physically possible to re-enact in the real world. Although someone may have a penchant for these infantilized baby animals, they are not real animals as they have been anthropomorphized. These are baby cartoon characters who can give affirmation that they are 'enjoying' the behaviour by speech or gesture, and that makes it very different from trying to perform an act of bestiality on a real baby animal. What is important, however, is to listen to Furries themselves: fandoms create boundaries and socially police what they find acceptable (Busse 2013).

Conclusion

It is important to talk about fandom pornography, not just for the Furry Fandom but for other fandoms as well. Although, others do not get as much as a severe backlash as Furry pornography, investigating these misconceptions can be helpful in destigmatizing these fandoms. As I have demonstrated in this chapter, Furry pornography does not indicate a sexual attraction to real-life animals and actually reinforces certain human aesthetics as to what should be considered attractive. This goes against research by Hsu and Bailey, who argued that 'male furries may also be both sexually attracted to real animals … because anthropomorphic and real animals are physically similar' (2019, 1360). This is not what I have found and have demonstrated this in my analysis of the great similarities between Furry pornography and human pornography.

I have identified the common motifs in Furry pornography related to those found in human pornography and found that these are commonly by 'perfect' genitalia and by adhering to common 'porn star' aesthetics such as massive breasts and penises. Furry pornography, and indeed fantasy pornography by extension, performs a function in allowing those with repressed non-heteronormative identities to be engaged with; Furries who feel unable to be homosexual or a different gender/fluid/non-binary in real life are able to live out this fantasy through their pornography away from social stigma.

Therefore, consuming Furry pornography is really not that different from consuming human pornography. In a way that is disappointing, because although the Furries are enacting a post-human identity, I have come to the conclusion that their pornography is edged closer to the human side. Although their pornography is post-human in the way that it engages with animal symbolism and has ramifications for companion species theory, from what I can surmise, the pleasure is coming distinctly from the human part of the symbiosis. In one way this is positive in as much as that means it is not bestiality, but it also means that Furries are still stuck with some ideas and values from our heterocentric society, even though their images have similarities with slash fandom that Booth (2014) has noted 'has the potential to subvert the patriarchy'. The majority of Furry pornography sadly does not seem to fulfil that function.

Strangely, pornography seems to be the only part of the fandom where hobbyists and lifestylers are doing something for the same reason. As I have shown through the other chapters in the book, they usually perform their fan activities for different reasons and at varying levels of identification. Conversely, there is no real distinction here which is why they were not separated in terms of theory when it came to this chapter.

7

Conclusion

The Furry Fandom is shifting with time. It shares many of the hallmarks of an institution as shown through fan policing of social behaviour like other fandoms, but it has no set text from which to draw these behaviours. For a Furry, their information about what it is to be a Furry can come from a variety of conflicting sources; the Furry Fandom has a hard challenge as they have more options to choose from when fans create their identity and not all Furries are choosing the same texts. As well as this, for some Furries, their Furry identity is part of themselves but is only enacted online rather than offline. However, I have attempted to address this in this book by using the breadth of identification between hobbyist and lifestyler.

When it comes to the fursona, many Furries in my study stated that they were using the species of their chosen fursona to personify certain personality traits that they themselves had or wished to be perceived as having. Thus far, there has been little analysis on why certain species are oversubscribed with the briefest of analysis given by Gerbasi et al. (2008, 198). I found that there are many reasons for quadrupeds to be chosen (especially fluffy ones) due to aesthetics and psychological reasons, but I also identified that pet ownership is a big influencing factor as well. This is possibly due to the Furry Fandom seeming to be a predominantly Western fandom and pet-keeping is often purely cultural, with Western countries far more likely to own a dog as a 'pet' rather than a working animal (Hogenboom 2015); as most of the people in my study come from Western countries where dogs are popular as pets, this could help explain why this popularity is transferred over to fursonas. Unfortunately, I had insufficient data to see whether the opposite was true, that is, if dogs were unpopular as fursonas in countries where culturally dogs are perceived as 'dirty'. But this would certainly be a good avenue for future research.

Another point of note that was outside the scope of my book but would be interesting for further research is reptilian fursonas. Although reptiles were unpopular in this study, Dragons (categorized as fictional/mythical creatures in this study) were somewhat popular in that they were often seen in mixed fursonas. These mythical creatures, including griffons and phoenixes, were almost as popular as feline fursonas. This is interesting as many of these animals are not 'furry' in the aesthetic sense but scaly or rough-skinned. There are reasons for this popularity that I have not quite figured out while writing this book, but I hypothesize that these will be related to myths we commonly hold about these beings.

IARP studies reviewed research which suggested that stigmatized communities have been researched over the years with the majority of them containing a biological or genetic component (Plante et al. 2014, 6). This is however highly contested through critiques of biological essentialism, and I did not see this fitting with the majority of Furries in my study. It has been noted that the 'perception of choice' means that some have trivialized chosen identities, such as fan membership (Chen 2007). This is despite evidence to show that it can be a very important or even integral part of someone's identity (Grossberg 1992; Wann and Branscombe 1993; Chen 2007). For Furries, stigmatization seems to come from the mass media and their spreading of negative stereotypes such as associations with bestiality. However, I have aimed to try and destigmatize at least the bestiality aspect with my analysis on Furry pornography where I found they have far more in common with human desires than animal.

One IARP study stated that 'approximately 50 % of Furries believe that their being Furry was not a choice' (Plante et al. 2014, 6). Their reference for this is unpublished raw data according to the bibliography and so cannot be confirmed. This also does not fit in with the Furries in my study as far as more Furries had a fan identity rather than one that was not chosen. The IARP did note that there are those who viewed Furry as being a choice, describing them as those 'who see the boundary between Furry and non-Furry as being more permeable' (ibid., 13) and these are the Furries who are just fans. However, in my book I have made sure to highlight the fact that they are perhaps the predominant group rather than a 50 per cent share. These Furries may see the identity as more easily concealed and so do not suffer the negative effects of doing so. This is thought-provoking because a point of contention in this study was the description of 'coming-out' when revealing to a non-Furry that they participate in the fandom; they do not see it as an identity and so do not want to be associated with high identifying members. However, this does not mean it is a choice or not, it means further study should be done to look at the implications within the fandom.

In this book, I have discussed cub fur, but there are several other categories that could become ethical and even legal quandaries. 'Feral' pornography is something that I have come across (though not when randomly selecting images for this study). In these categories, fursonas can sometimes be presented as non-anthropomorphic and so this could easily be construed by an outsider as a Furry enjoying animal sex. There are also categories which include rape fetishes and these should be included in research which has investigated rape fetishes (Horeck 2004). This is something that should be addressed in further research. However, I have offered up ideas that already can be applicable to other cartoon pornographies. In that my work has opened the Furry Fandom up to not be talked about or researched as a homogenous group as has previously been done. This means that more research can focus on how highly identified Furries are becoming post-human as well as being able to discuss less identified Furries within a fan studies theorem. I used this book to offer different ways to theorize fan erotica, particularly pairings involving animal characters. Due to the theoretical context of my study, which combines post-humanism and fan studies, I cite and analyse many pieces that would be relevant for being applied to hentai, which often has anthropomorphized monsters and fantasy characters. Consumers of hentai are also heavily stigmatized as having deviant fantasies, and the work on stigmatization can be applied to them also.

Although I very briefly mentioned Therians in this book, I have not placed them in a similar category to Furries even though work by Grivell et al. (2014) has placed these two groups together. The study by Grivell et al. (2014) uses the Furry typology used in Gerbasi et al. (2008). Grivell et al. suggest that Therians are similar to those participants in the Gerbasi et al. study as Therians 'considered themselves less than 100% human and would like to no longer be human' (2014, 114). Grivell et al. consider this to be where the Therians fit into the Furry Fandom as it seems to fit the definition for Therian when it comes to high identification. They also use the definition by Strill (2008) that a Therian is 'a person who is, feels, or believes he/she is in part or whole (non-physically) one or more non-human animals on an integral, personal level' (Grivell et al. 2014, 115).[1]

Using online interviews sourcing participants from a Therian web forum, they discovered that the Therians often described 'a long-term feeling of being somehow not quite human was described, coupled with expression of animal behaviours or mental states' (2014, 117). This could be revealed in experiencing phantom limbs and less commonly in experiencing mental shifts into the animal they identified with or 'theriotype' (ibid., 119).[2] Although many of these items are similar within some members of the Furry Fandom, they found that therianthropy 'came across as strongly as a personal identity rather than a group identity' (ibid., 121). This is very different from the community feeling found in studies specifically on Furries where it is often seen as both a personal and a group identity (Plante et al. 2014, 2015, 2016).

The main difference that can be taken from this study about the experiences of Furries and Therians is that Therians seem to heavily identify with the animal in a way that the majority of Furries do not. Although many Furries are spiritual (Plante et al. 2016, 16), Therians were more likely to endorse a biological component to their identity. Rather than a Therian's phantom limb experiences being simply in their imaginations 'the parallels to amputee phantom limbs suggests that these experiences may have some basis in a therian's biology' (Grivell et al. 2014, 128). For Grivell et al. this meant that the Therians felt there was a scientific explanation. The study by Grivell et al. suggests that Therians view being a Furry as a hobby or a lifestyle rather than something that was biologically determined compared to their Therian identity. This is the major point where Furries and Therians differ. Although the two groups may seem very similar to begin with, due to their interests in anthropomorphized animals, they are, in fact, different groups. The Grivell et al. study gives an insight into the ways in which Therians are both similar and also different from Furries, helping researchers not to get the communities confused. But this is also the reason why I did not speak about them in detail in my book.

Rukmini Pande has argued that fan studies has often 'ignored complex power relations within fan communities' and that racial divides in fandom are not covered (2018, 319). And a 'call to arms' to do more research on fans of colour was echoed by Stanfill: 'fans of color do of course exist in them, and the specificities of this dynamic need to be examined carefully' (Stanfill 2018, 307). This is something I have distinctly failed to interrogate in this book, and this is because, as Pande has noted, as a white scholar, it never occurred to me to look into these power relations, I did ignore them. This is something I would have done differently if I were to begin my research again, because demographically the Furry Fandom is predominantly white and there should be research as to why this is so. I only vaguely touched upon this in my book when it came to species choice. I argued that apes may be very rare as fursonas because of racist connotations of negatively relating apes to Black people (see Haraway 1991; Adams 2015). However, that does not explain why there are few Furries of colour in my statistics. This is something that is rich for future research and is something that I would suggest a scholar looks at first because, as Pande and Stanfill note, this type of research is lacking due to the whiteness of the scholars themselves.

Another aspect of the Furry Fandom which could use more research is that of economic capital. I briefly mentioned that Furries have typical fan practices such as shipping and creation of artworks, but there is also a gift economy present as well. A gift economy is where fans distribute their own fan works for free rather than asking for monetary payment, for example, free access for those who want to view their fan fiction or homemade artwork. Karen Hellekson lists two main reasons for this: many fans keep their work free due to fears of being sued for copyright infringement; and it keeps fan communities exclusive giving fandoms their 'own autonomy while simultaneously solidifying the group' (2009, 114–17). Scott (2009) expresses her concerns 'on flagrant instances of the industry's attempt to co-opt fandom' in that they do not consider that fan value creation is not new. Stanfill certainly agrees with this, asserting that fandom, like other institutions, 'has never been isolated from market values' (2013b).

In a way, the Furries are slightly more protected from these market values because there is not a company (due to no set media text) to swoop in and profit from their fan-made material. However, the Furry Fandom have created their own capitalist economy whereby those with talents gain monetary commissions for fan artwork and fursuits. Anne Gilbert noted that by using economic capital, fans can boost their social capital and possibly push themselves up the fan hierarchy:

> Exclusive content, merchandise, and celebrity interaction are incentives that generate positive social capital among fans while reinforcing consumptive practices that have economic benefits for industry producers. (2017, 359)

I have used the concept of the habitus to explain how Furries create their community online when it comes to their identity and how they share cultural capital. Therefore, investigation into the economic capital would be very useful in fleshing out this idea. Especially because there are so many Furries in my study who are envious of those who have a fursuit and due to the majority of Furries who would like a fursuit but cannot afford one; an investigation into the fan dynamics this creates would be welcome.

In conclusion, the Furries that make up the Furry Fandom are not a homogenous group. For better or worse, they encompass many of the difficulties that come with other fandoms; they are stigmatized by the media; they sometimes stigmatize themselves; and sometimes 'policing' goes too far. However, they also share the positives that come from being in a fandom. Furries in my study related much of their well-being to having like-minded people to talk to and a community they could be involved in online when their 'real life' was getting too much. The Furry Fandom has been growing since the late 1980s, and it does not look like that growth will be stopping any time soon. Hopefully, this means that the general public will be able to refrain from bringing up 'uncertain references' to popular culture when asked about who and what Furries are (Soh and Cantor 2015, 1).

Glossary

Anthropomorphics

The adjective is used in two ways to describe human and non-human characteristics. Anthropomorphic can be used to explain animal behaviour in human terms, that is, 'the dog is looking guilty because he was naughty'. It can also be used to describe an animal having human characteristics. In the Furry Fandom this is where their drawing may include animals in clothes or drinking coffee.

Brony

Bronies are a subgroup related to the Furry Fandom who particularly place their emphasis on the pony characters from *My Little Pony: Friendship Is Magic*. They exclusively use pony fursonas rather than other species and take many of their fan ideas from the show rather than the Furry Fandom at large.

Cub Fur

Cub furs are a controversial part of the Furry Fandom as these are typically fursonas or fursuits that depict a newborn/infant version of the animal species that are being portrayed. Although many portrayals of baby Furries are usually benign and often meant to be cute, there are some who draw baby or cub fursonas in sexually explicit scenarios. This can cause issues for some as they view baby furs as being underage and so associate a sexually explicit Baby Fur artwork as being paedophilic in nature.

Fur Meets

This is the informal term that many Furries use to describe their offline meet ups with other Furries. These events are often an opportunity to show off full and partial fursuits and to catch up with friends. A common practice at these events is to wear a lanyard with pictures portraying their fursona or their Furry name.

Fursecution

A semi-serious term used by members of the fandom to describe how they may feel persecuted particularly for being a Furry. This term has become popular to describe unsavoury and uncomplimentary media coverage – for example, when Mika Brzezinski laughed and ran off stage when discussing the chlorine gas attack on the Midwest Furfest in 2014, despite the fact that nineteen Furries had been hospitalized during the incident and the use of chlorine gas is considered a war crime or terrorist act. Furries often view this incident as an example of Fursecution because although a serious crime has been committed and people have been injured, it is seen as a joke simply because they are Furries.

Fursuits

Fursuits are suits that a Furry can wear, which is usually of their fursona. A full fursuit will contain full body covering including a head, though it is not uncommon to see Furries wearing ears and/or a furry tail if they do not wish to wear a full suit. Fursuits, although being a popular stereotype that a lay person will come up with when asked about Furries, are actually not that common. There is evidence to show that many Furries would like to own a fursuit given the chance, but due to the very high cost in making these custom suits (usually running into the thousands) many Furries will not own one.

There are three different main categories of fur suits: 'toony' suits which are designed to be cartoon-like, usually with large eyes and neon colours; 'realistic' suits which are designed to look anatomically similar to the animal on which they are based; and then the rarer 'quad suit' made for the purpose of being able to walk on all fours.

Fursona

A fursona is a representation of the Furries' anthropomorphic persona which are usually drawn by the Furry themselves or commissioned by an artist. Fursonas have previously been viewed as an important identifying feature of being a Furry with some studies showing that more than 95 per cent of Furries have at least one fursona.

Grey Muzzle

A term that is typically used by or referred to by older members of the fandom. Typically, it denotes those who have been in the fandom for an extended period or are simply older than the average Furry, which is predominantly under the age of 25. The phrase originally meant to refer to those who were Furries in the pre-internet era but has evolved to include other demographics as well.

Therian

Therians are a group related to the Furry Fandom, and often mistaken for Furries, who experience a very high level of connection with their fursona in that they perceive their fursona to be a part of their psyche. Therians range from those who feel that they have been born in the wrong body and should have actually been their fursonas to those who experience 'mental shifts' into their fursonas and so have the feeling of phantom ears and tails.

Vore

Vore is a category within Furry Fandom pornography which depicts a fursona eating another fursona as part of sexual gratification. Representations of vore can include a cross-section of the 'inside' of the fursona's stomach to show the fursona that has been eaten being digested. Vore can be perceived as deviant, even within the Furry Fandom, as it has been seen as akin to promoting cannibalism.

Yiff

The word yiff is slang which has common usage in the Furry fandom and is used as 'a catchall term for nearly anything pornographic in nature within the fandom'. Although the origin of the word is unclear, it is noted as being similar to the sound a fox makes in real life, reflecting foxes as a very common fursona species. Furry-specific sexual slang terms are in common use; Murr is also a slang word used in the Furry Fandom that denotes sexual pleasure in role play. Unfortunately, as the term Yiff has become known to those outside the fandom, it is now also being used to insult members of the fandom by outsiders, most commonly used in the phrase 'Yiff in Hell'.

Notes

1 Introduction: The Furry Fandom

1 These statistics can be found on the Wikifur archive online.
2 If you have not done so, it may be helpful for you to read through the glossary, which gives a breakdown of many Furry Fandom–related terms.
3 *My Little Pony: Friendship Is Magic* ran on the Hub Network from 2010 to 2014 before being moved to Discovery Family until the show ended in October 2019. This reboot was incredibly popular and has continued to be a progressive and involved fandom even after the show ended.
4 These polls by AdjectiveSpecies can be found on their Twitter (of the same name) and Wordpress pages.
5 This is also from AdjectiveSpecies from their poll in 2017.
6 Reddit Blogs provide comprehensive statistics and demographics each year and shows their active users have remained stable for the last few years, providing a rich potential data set for researchers.
7 The IARP have published some findings on their website FurScience; however, these are limited to a webpage of presentation of findings rather than a peer-reviewed analysis.

2 Furries as fans

1 A term used to describe erotica (usually homosexual) between two fictional characters who were not sexual/romantic in the original text.
2 In recent years, the term 'Mary Sue' has come to mean a character who is too perfect to be believable (Austin 2018, 56). Mary Sue is often seen as a negative term in which fan writers imbue their original characters with 'unrealistic' powers that always save the day. However, this term is also predominantly used by male writers critiquing female stories so this may be more indicative of sexism than real literary critique.
3 *Twilight* is the first book of the Twilight series written by Stephanie Meyer (2008). The books are centred around a love triangle which blossoms over the series between a girl, Bella, and Edward and Jacob. This led to some fans being 'Team

Edward' or 'Team Jacob' and this gained the ire of mainly male fans. This is similar to the way that female fans have been viewed over the decades as being too 'romantic' or too identifying with their fan object because male fans seem to think they have more subjectivity in these matters.

4 See Jenkins (2006), Johnson (2007) and Scodari (2007) for further information about negative reactions to fan policing.

5 This is important within fan studies as many popular fandom identities are sci-fi or supernatural in basis; fan identity based on impossibilities seem to be a crucial identifier.

6 Gender identity disorder is often viewed as a politically incorrect term in more recent years. This is because it infers that transgender people have a mental illness.

7 Speciesist/speciesism is the assumption of human superiority leading to the exploitation of animals.

3 The Furry habitus

1 Pierre Bourdieu's concept of the habitus is described in depth in Chapter 2 – 'Furries as fans'.

2 MSNBC aired footage of news anchors laughing when reporting on the chemical attack. This was considered as particularly heinous because the use of chlorine gas against civilians is considered a war crime by the Hague.

3 This 9 per cent came from 1,000 responses.

4 I ran a chi-squared test which shows a significant result between age and Furry internet consumption showing that there is a high probability that these two variables are related.

5 To be discussed further in Chapter 5 on stigmatization.

6 See Costa et al. (2000), McCrae and Costa (1999).

7 See Jenkins et al. (2012), Reynolds et al. (2010, 2012), Turner and Onorato (1999).

8 This statement occurs because Walter feels people are not paying attention to the rules of bowling and draws a gun at this point. The overreaction of Walter is considered a pivotal comedic scene which is probably why it lends itself to memes so well.

9 See Rudwick and Ntuli (2009), Blake (2010, 136).

10 Flaming is the act of posting or sending offensive messages over the internet to provoke a negative reaction.

11 See Long and Chen (2007), Ridout et al. (2012), Radovic et al. (2017), Chou and Edge (2012).

4 Species choice in the Furry Fandom

1 QI did an interesting segment on how repulsed cockroaches are by humans in an episode in 2018.

2 It should be noted here that this was archetype worship in that cats were not exalted as gods but were killed in worshipping practices.

3 In reference to the internet sensation and real-life feline Grumpy Cat (real name is Tardar Sauce) whose photo of her looking particularly grumpy sparked a viral meme with the cat ending up with her own movie on Lifetime. Although, she has since passed away – her owners still keep a hugely subscribed-to media account using old photos and competitions to keep consumers following. A popular internet meme which is usually with a picture background of a domesticated cat with the words, spoken by the cat (misspelt of course) 'I can has Cheezburger?'

4 Acronym – r/furryinreallife.

5 I found that in my research, eventually owning a fursuit was something that many Furries stated as an aspiration. This is despite my study revealing that only 8 per cent of Furries owned a full suit – this may be because they are seen as a status symbol in the fandom due to the cost of making one.

6 Autopoiesis is used here in the philosophical sense in that opinions are not 'self-making' and influenced by outside forces rather than the literal biological process in living cells being self-sustaining (Haraway 2008, 32).

7 For lifestylers, they do not anthropomorphize the animal and so although they may be influenced by some myth, they are more similar to the post-human.

8 Synopsis: *Zootopia* is an anthropomorphic film starring a bunny called Judy Hopps who wishes to become the first rabbit police officer in the capital city of Zootopia. Judy struggles to be accepted by other members of the police force as they are much bigger and 'stronger' animals such as bison, cheetahs and elephants. While on duty she meets a con artist fox called Nick Wilde who hustles her, she later relies on his help to solve fourteen missing animal cases.

9 There are many versions of *Reynard the Fox*, but the reference used is of the oldest and most extensive first use of the character.

10 The movie performed modestly at the box office, only earning $21 million on a film budget of $8 million. The film currently sits at 58 per cent fresh rating on Rotten Tomatoes, which is a mixed reception.

11 Steven Stern, 'Bright Eyes', *Frieze*, XLV (1999), pp. 45–6 – When trying to find the original work by Stern it was not available on any of the university databases I had access to. As well as this, the citation only produced eight results in a Google search when I first searched for it in 2016. Out of the eight results, six were unrelated and

two were referencing the citation in Baker's book. This strengthens the argument made here that many references to Furries in academia, postmodern art and popular culture are often based on references which are incorrect or lacking in background.

5 Stigmatization in the Furry Fandom

1 See Spencer et al. (1999), Steele and Aronson (1995) and Hess et al. (2003).
2 See glossary for fursecution definition.
3 See also Ellemers et al. (2002), Jetten et al. (2001), Spears et al. (1997).
4 Waifu – A fictional character that is treated and spoken about like a wife to the real person. A popular way to express the fact that one has a waifu is to buy a life-size pillow with the character appearance.
5 Once again we see the prevailing stereotype for Furries being 'Furries are employed in computer or science fields' as noted by Gerbasi et al. in their seminal study (2008, 204).
6 This is less about writers trying to be sympathetic to Furries in their subject matter but more to do with the conventions of CSI in general. A common theme is that the head scientist is old, male and white and shows more objectivity than other team members (Jenner 2016).
7 In their study, Roberts et al. (2015b) investigated whether Furries disclosed their identity when visiting a doctor/clinician for 'unrelated conditions'. They did this as they hypothesized that Furries would gain better healthcare from their provider if they felt comfortable disclosing their Furry identity, especially if the clinicians had some knowledge of the fandom.
8 *1000 Ways to Die* (McMahon 2008–12) showed an episode (1/4) where a man dies after coming across a Furry 'orgy'. He tried to join into the orgy, but was rebuffed, and then mistook a nearby brown bear as a human participant; he was then mauled to death.

6 Pornography in the Furry Fandom

1 I collected data on artwork during 2009–12 from Furaffinity.com to see total submissions (and subsequently published) of artwork and over those years 'mature' labelled artwork never saw a submission rate of more than 10 per cent. When I was writing this book, I went to other websites and back to Furaffinity and found

that this rate of submission has not increased by a large margin and pornographic submissions are still very much in the minority.

2   Autoanthropomorphozoophilia is the term given by Hsu and Bailey for a sexual attraction to anthropomorphic animals.

3   Yaoi – also known as 'Boy Love' – focuses on romantic or sexual relationships between male characters, typically aimed at a female audience and usually created by female authors. Shojo – this manga has a variety of narrative styles, from historical drama to science fiction, often with a focus on romantic relationships or emotions. It is particularly targeted at a young female demographic.

4   See also Durham (2015, 2), Clover (1993, 1) and Ellis (1992, 147).

5   At the SAMLA conference in Alabama in 2018, I presented a paper on transgenderism in the Furry Fandom. I could not go into the pornography representations due to time limitations, but I want to emphasis again, how important it can be for those who are not able to live as trans in 'real life' can find a catharsis by enacting it on paper, and this certainly extends to sexual relief as well.

6   I argue that there are specific cultural reasons for why dogs in particular are chosen in Chapter 4. Essentially, when you grow up with positive dog role models like Lassie, Beethoven, Air Bud and Bolt, these are more likely to transfer over into what you find aesthetically pleasing when you pick a character to represent yourself.

7   It is worth noting that in recent years there has been a distinct change in cartoons and I am thankful to say that many have become far more diverse. Programs such as *Steven Universe*, *Shera and the Princesses of Power* and *Kipo and the Age of Wonderbeasts* have changed the landscape of family television and have become incredibly popular; they have excellent storylines and also make a conscious effort to include central characters of different races, genders and sexualities, far more than would have been seen in the early 2000s and 1990s when I grew up.

8   This is a notion put forward by Deleuze and Guattari in how nature and technology combine.

9   In the data from where this chapter is derived, I used multiple pictures to show different erotic scenes from Furry pornography and analysed them. I did not include pictures in this book due to copyright (and also not wanting to make the book more expensive!). This was because I asserted at the time, and still assert now, that I would have been sharing images of child pornography which is why I omitted any of those images from my thesis.

7 Conclusion

1   The Strill (2008) reference used by Grivell et al. (2014) now leads to a defunct
    website (http://project-shift.net/are-you-a-therian/), so we can no longer see what
    other information on Therian's was available at the time of their research.
2   Theriotype – the type of animal with which they 'shift' into, similar to lycanthropy
    but not restricted to the wolf species.

Bibliography

Adams, Carol J. 1995. 'Woman Battering and Harm to Animals', in *Animals and Women: Feminist Theoretical Explorations*, edited by Carol J. Adams and Josephine Donovan, 55–84, Durham, NC: Duke University Press.

Adams, Carol J. 2006. 'An Animal Manifesto Gender, Identity, and Vegan-Feminism in the Twenty-First Century: An Interview with Carol J. Adams', *Parallax* 12, 1:120–8.

Adams, Carol J. 2015. *Neither Man nor Beast: Feminism and the Defence of Animals*, New York: Lantern Books.

Aesop. 620–564 BCE. *The Ass in the Lion's Skin*, Greece: Perry Index.

Aesop. 620–564 BCE. *The Fox and the Stork*, Greece: Collection of Phaedrus.

Alexander, Jeffery C. 2004. 'Towards a Theory of Cultural Trauma', in *Cultural Trauma and Collective Identity*, edited by Jeffery C. Alexander, Ron Eyerman, Bernhard Giesen, Neil J. Smelser and Piotr Sztompka, 1–30, Berkeley: University of California Press.

Althusser, Louis. 1971. *Essays on Ideology*, London: Verso.

Androutsopoulos, Jannis K., and Georgeakopolous, Alexandra. 2003. 'Discourse Construction of Youth Identities: Introduction', in *Discourse Construction of Youth Identities*, edited by Jannis K. Androutsopoulos and Alexandra Georgeakopolous, 1–25, Amsterdam: John Benjamin's.

APA. 2012. 'The Minority Stress Perspective', *American Psychology Association*, April 2012. http://www.apa.org/pi/aids/resources/exchange/2012/04/minority-stress.aspx.

Apted, Michael. 1988. *Gorillas in the Mist* (film), Universal City, CA: Universal Pictures/ Warner Bros. Pictures.

Asquith, Daisy. 2013. *Crazy about One Direction* (television documentary), UK: Channel 4.

Attwood, Fiona. 2011. 'The Paradigm Shift: Pornography Research, Sexualization and Extreme Images', *Sociology Compass* 5, 1:13–22.

Attwood, Fiona. 2014. 'Immersion: "Extreme" Texts, Animated Bodies and the Media', *Media, Culture and Society* 36, 8:1186–95.

Austin, Jessica. 2017. 'Online Hate and Hurt: Ethical Considerations When Online Research Takes an Ugly Turn', *Nordic Journal of Information Science and Cultural Mediation* 6, 1:1–16.

Austin, Jessica. 2018. '"Fan Girls Going Rogue": The Reception of the Force Awakens and Rogue One with Female Fans', *Kinephanos: Journal of Media Studies and Popular Culture* 8, 1:46–66.

Bacon-Smith, Camille. 1992. *Enterprising Women: Television Fandom and the Creation of Popular Myth*, Philadelphia: University of Pennsylvania Press.

Bannon, Katie L., Hunter-Reel, Dorian, Wilson, G. Terence, and Karlin, Robert A. 2009. 'The Effects of Causal Beliefs and Binge Eating on the Stigmatization of Obesity', *International Journal of Eating Disorders* 42, 2:118–24.

Baker, Steven. 2000. *The Postmodern Animal*, London: Reakiton Books.

Barker, Martin, and Mathjis, Ernest. 2008. *Watching the Lord of the Rings: Tolkien's World Audiences*, New York: Peter Lang.

Barthes, Roland. 1957. *Mythologies*, London: Vintage Books.

Baym, Nancy. 2000. *Tune in, Log on: Soaps, Fandom and Online Community*, New York: Sage.

Baym, Nancy. 2015. *Personal Connections in the Digital Age, Digital Media and Society Series*, London: Polity Press.

Bednarek, Joanna. 2017. 'The Oedipal Animal? Companion Species and Becoming', in *Deleuze and the Animal*, edited by Colin Gardner and Patricia MacCormack, 52–74, Edinburgh: Edinburgh University Press.

Bell, Christopher. 2013. 'The Ballad of Derpy Hooves – Transgressive Fandom in *My Little Pony: Friendship Is Magic*', *Humanities Directory* 1, 1:5–22.

Blake, Barry J. 2010. *Secret Language*, Oxford: Oxford University Press.

Booth, Paul. 2010. *Digital Fandom: New Media Studies*, Switzerland: Peter Lang.

Booth, Paul. 2014. '292 and Porn: Media Subversion, Hyper-Articulation, and Parody', *Journal of Media and Cultural Studies* 28, 3:396–409.

Booth, Paul. 2018. *A Companion to Media Fandom and Fan Studies*, edited by Paul Booth. New York: Wiley Blackwell.

Booth, Paul, and Kelly, Peter. 2013. 'The Changing Faces of Doctor Who Fandom: New Fans, New Technologies, Old Practices?', *Participations: Journal of Audience and Reception Studies* 10, 1:56–72.

Bourdieu, Pierre. 1977. *Outline of a Theory of Practice*, Cambridge: Cambridge University Press.

Bourdieu, Pierre. 1984. *Distinction: A Social Critique of the Judgement of Taste*, Cambridge, MA: Harvard University Press.

Bradshaw, John. 2011. *In Defence of Dogs*, London: Penguin Books.

Branscombe, Nyla R., Schmitt, Michael T., and Harvey, Richard D. 1999. 'Perceiving Pervasive Discrimination among African Americans: Implications for Group Identification and Well-Being', *Journal of Personality and Social Psychology* 77:135–49.

Branscombe, Nyla R., Mavor, Ken, and Batalha, Luisa. 2012. 'Social Identity and Personality Processes: Non-Aboriginal Australian Identity and Neuroticism', *European Journal of Social Psychology* 42:252–62.

Bryant, Clifton, D., and Forsyth, Craig J. 2021. 'The Complexity of Deviant Lifestyles', *Deviant Behavior* 33, 7:525–49.

Bryman, Alan. 2012. *Social Research Methods*, Oxford: Oxford University Press.

Burgess, Jean. 2006. 'Hearing Ordinary Voices: Cultural Studies, Vernacular Creativity and Digital Storytelling', *Continuum: Journal of Media and Cultural Studies* 20, 2:201–14.

Burton, Tim. (Director). 2001. *Planet of the Apes* (film), United States: 20th Century Fox.

Busse, Kristina. 2013. 'Geek Hierarchies, Boundary Policing, and the Gendering of the Good Fan', *Participations: Journal of Audience and Reception Studies* 10, 1:73–9.

Butler, Judith. 1990. *Gender Trouble: Feminism and the Subversion of Identity*, London: Routledge.

Butler, Judith. 1993. *Bodies That Matter*, London: Routledge.

Calarco, Matthew. 2008. *Zoographies: The Question of the Animal from Heidegger to Derrida*, New York: Columbia University Press.

Carlson, Marla. 2011. 'Furry Cartography: Performing Species', *Theatre Journal* 63, 2:191–208.

Carrington, Victoria. 2005. 'New Textual Landscapes, Information and Early Literacy', in *Popular Culture, New Media and Digital Literacy in Early Childhood*, edited by Jackie Marsh, 13–30, Oxon, UK: Routledge.

Carroll, Lewis. 1865. *Alice's Adventures in Wonderland*, London: Macmillan.

Chen, Jin-Shiow. 2007. 'A Study of Fan Culture: Adolescent Experiences with Animé/ Manga Doujinshi and Cosplay in Taiwan', *Visual Arts Research* 33:14–24.

Chou, Hui-Tzu, and Edge, Grace. 2012. '"They Are Happier and Having Better Lives Than I Am": The Impact of Using Facebook on Perceptions of Others' Lives', *Cyberpsychology Behavior and Social Networking* 15, 2:117–21.

Chouliaraki, Lilie. 2013. 'Mediated Experience and Youth Identities in a Post-Traditional Order', in *Discourse Construction of Youth Identities*, edited by Jannis K. Androutsopoulos and Alexandra Georgeakopolous, 303–31, Amsterdam: John Benjamins.

Clover, Carol. 1993. 'Introduction', in *Dirty Looks: Women, Pornography, Power*, edited by Pamela Church Gibson and Roma Gibson, 1–5, London: BFI Publishing.

Coon Sells, Tamara G. 2013. 'The Construction of Sexual Identities in an Online Gay, Lesbian, and Bisexual Bulletin Board System', *Journal of Human Behaviour in the Social Environment* 23, 8:893–907.

Cooper, Joanne, Brandon, Paul, and Lindberg, Marlene. 1997. *Using Peer Debriefing in the Final Stage of Evaluation with Implications for Qualitative Research: Three Impressionist Tales*, Chicago, IL: Annual Meeting of the American Educational Research Association.

Coppa, Francesca. 2014. 'Fuck Yeah, Fandom Is Beautiful', *Journal of Fandom Studies* 2, 1:73–82.

Costa, Paul T., Herbst, Jeffrey H., McCrae, Robert R., and Siegler, Ilene C. 2000. 'Personality at Midlife: Stability, Intrinsic Maturation, and Response to Life Event', *Assessment* 7, 4:365–78.

Cox, Christoph. 2005. 'Of Humans, Animals, and Monsters', in Becoming Animal: *Contemporary Art in the Animal Kingdom*, edited by Nato Thompson and Christoph Cox, 14–32, North Adams, MA: Mass MoCA Publications.

Crocker, Jennifer, Major, Brenda, and Steele, Claude. 1998. 'Social Stigma', in *The Handbook of Social Psychology*, edited by Daniel Todd Gilbert, Susan T. Fiske and Gardner Lidzey, 50–3. Boston, MA: Mcgraw-Hill.

Dank, Barry M. 1975. 'Coming Out in the Gay World', in *Deviance: Studies in Definition, Management and Treatment*, edited by Russell Rowe Dynes, Alfred Carpenter Clarke and Simon Dinitz, 215–51. Oxford: Oxford University Press.

Deleuze, Gilles. 2003. *Francis Bacon: The Logic of Sensation*, London: Continuum.

Deleuze, Gilles. 2004. *The Logic of Sense*, London: Bloomsbury Academic.

Deleuze, Gilles. 2014. *Difference and Repetition*, London: Bloomsbury Academic.

Deleuze, Gilles, and Guattari, Félix. 2013a. *A Thousand Plateaus*, London: Bloomsbury Academic.

Deleuze, Gilles, and Guattari, Félix. 2013b. *Anti-Oedipus*, London: Bloomsbury Academic.

Deller, Ruth A. 2018. 'Ethics in Fan Studies Research', in *A Companion to Media Fandom and Fan Studies*, edited by Paul Booth, 123–43. New York: Wiley Blackwell.

Derrida, Jacques, and Willis, David. 2002. 'The Animal That Therefore I Am (More to Follow)', *Critical Inquiry* 28, 2:369–418.

De Saint-Cloud, Pierre. 1170. *Le Roman de Renart*, France: unknown publisher.

Driscoll, Catherine. 2006. 'One True Pairing: The Romance of Pornography and the Pornography of Romance', in *Fan Fiction and Fan Communities in the Age of the Internet: New Essays*, edited by Karen Hellekson and Kristina Busse, 79–97. Jefferson, NC: McFarland.

Duffett, Mark. 2013. *Understanding Fandom: An Introduction to the Study of Media Fan Culture*, New York: Bloomsbury Academic.

Durham, Sarah. 2015. *Opposing Pornography: A Look at the Anti-Pornography Movement*. United States: Lulu.com.

Ellemers, Naomi, Spears, Russell, and Doosje, Bertjan. 2002. 'Self and Social Identity', *Annual Review of Psychology* 53:161–86.

Ellin. Doug. 2004–11. *Entourage* (television series), United States: HBO.

Ellis, John. 1992. 'On Pornography', in *The Sexual Subject: A Screen Reader in Sexuality*, edited by John Caughie and Annette Kuhn, 146–70, London: Routledge.

Erikson, Erik H. 1968. *Identity, Youth and Crisis*, New York: W. W. Norton.

Ferreday, Debra. 2011. 'Becoming Deer: Nonhuman Drag and Online Utopias', *Feminist Theory* 12, 2:219–25.

Fey, Tina. 2006–13. *30 Rock* (television series), United States: NBC.

Fisher, John A. 2005. 'High Art Versus Low Art', in *The Routledge Companion to Aesthetics*, edited by Berys Gaut and Dominic McIver Lopes, 527–40, London: Routledge.

Foucault, Michel. 1984a. 'Truth and Power', in *The Foucault Reader*, edited by Paul Rabinow, 51–75, England: Clays.

Foucault, Michel. 1984b. 'The Means of Correct Training', in *The Foucault Reader*, edited by Paul Rabinow, 188–205, England: Clays.

Freud, Sigmund. 2003. 'Consciousness and What Is Unconscious', in *Identities: Race, Class, Gender and Nationality*, edited by Linda Martin Alcoff and Eduardo Mendieta, 29–31, London: Blackwell.

Friese, Heidrun. 2002. 'Identity: Desire, Name and Difference', in *Identities: Time, Difference and Boundaries*, edited by Heidrun Friese, 17–31, Germany: Berghahn Books.

Frosh, Stephen. 1991. *Identity Crisis: Modernity, Psychoanalysis and the Self*, Great Britain: Palgrave Macmillan.

Frost, John. 2016, 'How Zootopia Was Made, Talking with Disney's Animation Team', *The Disney Blog*, 2 March 2016. http://thedisneyblog.com/2016/03/02/how-zootopia-was-made-talking-with-disneys-animation-team/.

Garcia, Angela Cora, Standlee, Alecea I., Bechkoff, Jennifer, and Cui, Yan. 2009. 'Ethnographic Approaches to the Internet and Computer-Mediated Communication', *Journal of Contemporary Ethnography* 38, 1:52–84.

Gardner, Colin, and MacCormack, Patricia. 2017. 'Introduction', in *Deleuze and the Animal*, edited by Colin Gardner and Patricia MacCormack, 1–34, Edinburgh: Edinburgh University Press.

Gatson, Sarah N., and Reid, Robin Anne. 2012. 'Race and Ethnicity in Fandom', *Journal of Transformative Works* 8, 1:n.p.

Gauntlett, David. 2008. *Media, Gender and Identity: An Introduction*, London: Routledge.

Geraghty, Lincoln. 2014. *Cult Collectors: Nostalgia, Fandom and Collecting Popular Culture*, London: Routledge.

Gerbasi, Kathleen C., Paolone, Nicholas, Higner, Justin, Scaletta, Laura L., Bernstein, Penny L., Conway, Samuel, and Privitera, Adam John. 2008. 'Furries from A to Z (Anthropomorphism to Zoomorphism)', *Society and Animals* 16:197–222.

Gerbasi, Kathleen C., Scaletta, Laura L., Plante, Courtney N., and Bernstein, Penny L. 2011. 'Why so FURious? Rebuttal of Dr. Fiona Probyn-Rapsey's Response to Gerbasi et al.'s Furries from A to Z (Anthropomorphism to Zoomorphism)', *Society and Animals* 19, 3:302–4.

Giddens, Anthony. 1991. *Modernity and Self-Identity: Self and Society in the Late Modern Age*, Palo Alto, CA: Stanford University Press.

Giffney, Noreen. 2009. 'The New Queer Cartoon', in *The Ashgate Research Companion to Queer Theory*, edited by Noreen Giffney and Michael O'Rourke, Chapter 22, Farnham, UK: Ashgate.

Gilbert, Anne. 2017. 'Live from Hall H: Fan/Producer Symbiosis at San Diego Comic-Con', in *Fandom, Second Edition: Identities and Communities in a Mediated World*, edited by Jonathan Gray, Cornell Sandvoss and C. Lee Harrington, 354–68, New York: New York University Press.

Goffman, Erving. 1959. *The Presentation of Self in Everyday Life*, New York: Penguin.

Gold, Kyell. 2015. 'Furry Erotica', in *Furries Among Us: Essays on Furries by the Most Prominent Members of the Fandom*, edited by Thurston Howl, 28–34, Nashville, TN: Thurston Howl Publications.

Grey, Terrance B. 2020. 'Furry Sexuality: Conditioned Fetishes a Better Explanation Than Erotic Target Identity Inversion', *Archives of Sexual Behavior* 49:49–52.

Grivell, Timothy, Clegg, Helen, and Roxburgh, Elizabeth C. 2014. 'An Interpretative Phenomenological Analysis of Identity in the Therian Community, Identity', *An International Journal of Theory and Research* 14, 2:113–35.

Grossberg, Lawrence. 1992. 'Is There a Fan in the House?: The Affective Sensibility of Fandom', in *The Adoring Audience: Fan Culture and Popular Media*, edited by Laura A. Lewis, 50–68, London: Routledge.

Grossman, Arnold H., and Kerner, Matthew S. 1998. 'Self-Esteem and Supportiveness as Predictors of Emotional Distress in Gay Male and Lesbian Youth', *Journal of Homosexuality* 35:25–39.

Guattari, Félix. 2015. *Psychoanalysis and Tranversality: Texts and Interviews 1955-1971*, South Pasadena, CA: Semiotext(e).

Gurley, George. 2001. 'Pleasures of the Fur', *Vanity Fair*, March. https://archive.vanityfair.com/article/2001/3/pleasures-of-the-fur.

Haenfler, Ross. 2010. Goths, Gamers and Grrrl: Deviance and Youth Subcultures. Oxford: Oxford University Press.

Haraway, Donna. 1989. *Primate Visions: Gender, Race and Nature in the World of Modern Science*, New York: Routledge.

Haraway, Donna. 1991. *Simians, Cyborgs, and Women: The Reinvention of Nature*, Great Britain: Free Association Books.

Haraway, Donna. 2003. *The Companion Species Manifesto*, Chicago: Prickly Paradigm Press.

Haraway, Donna. 2008. *When Species Meet*, Minneapolis, MN: University of Minnesota Press.

Haraway, Donna. 2016. *Staying with the Trouble: Making Kin in the Chthulucene*, Durham, NC: Duke University Press.

Harper, Stephen. 2009. *Madness, Power and the Media: Class, Gender, and Race in Popular Representations of Mental Distress*, London: Palgrave MacMillan.

Hecht, Julie, and Horowitz, Alexandra. 2015. 'Seeing Dogs: Human Preferences for Dog Physical Attributes', *Anthrozoös* 28, 1:153–63.

Hebdige, Dick. 2003. 'Disgnosis: Disney and the Retooling of Knowledge, Art, Culture, Life, Etc.' *Cultural Studies* 17, 2:150–67.

Hegel, Georg Wilhelm Friedrich. 2003. 'Independence and Dependence of Self-Consciousness', in *Identities: Race, Class, Gender and Nationality*, edited by Linda Martin Alcoff and Eduardo Mendieta, 11–16, London: Blackwell.

Hellekson, Karen. 2009. 'A Fannish Field of Value: Online Fan Gift Culture', *Cinema Journal* 48, 4:113–18.

Hess, Thomas M., Auman, Corinne, Colcombe, Stanley J., and Rahhal, Tamara A. 2003. 'The Impact of Stereotype Threat on Age Differences in Memory Performance', *Journals of Gerontology* 58, 1:3–11.

Hills, Matt. 2002. *Fan Cultures*, London: Routledge.

Hills, Matt. 2014. 'Doctor Who's Textual Commemorators: Fandom, Collective Memory and the Self-Commodification of Fanfic', *Journal of Fandom Studies* 2, 1:31–51.

Hird, Myra J. 2009. 'Biologically Queer', in *The Ashgate Research Companion to Queer Theory*, edited by Noreen Giffney and Michael O'Rourke, 347–62, Farnham, UK: Ashgate.

Hogenboom, Melissa. 2015. 'Why Do We Love Our Pets So Much?', *BBC Earth*, 29 May 2015. http://www.bbc.co.uk/earth/story/20150530-why-do-we-love-our-pets-so-much.

Hong, Fu-Yuan., Huang, Der-Hsiang., Lin, Hung-Yu, and Chiu, Su-Lin. 2014. 'Analysis of the Psychological Traits, Facebook Usage, and Facebook Addiction Model of Taiwanese University Students', *Telematics and Informatics* 31, 4:597–606.

Horeck, Tanya. 2004. *Public Rape: Representing Violation in Fiction and Film*, London: Routledge.

Howl, Thurston. 2015. 'Yiff? Murr?: Sex in the Furry Fandom', in *Furries Among Us: Essays on Furries by the Most Prominent Members of the Fandom*, edited by Thurston Howl, 48–53, Nashville. TN: Thurston Howl Publications.

Hsu, Kevin J., and Bailey, Michael J. 2019. 'The "Furry" Phenomenon: Characterizing Sexual Orientation, Sexual Motivation, and Erotic Target Identity Inversions in Male Furries', *Archives of Sexual Behavior* 48:1349–69.

Hypetaph. 2015. 'The Furry Fandom as a Folk Group', in *Furries Among Us: Essays on Furries by the Most Prominent Members of the Fandom*, edited by Thurston Howl, 18–27, Nashville. TN: Thurston Howl Publications.

IARP. 2017. 'Minorities within a Minority, Face Recognition, and Furry Pornography', *Anthropomorphic Research Project*. https://sites.google.com/site/anthropomorphicresearch/past-results/furry-fiesta-2015.

Jacobs, Arthur P. (Producer). 1968–73. *Planet of the Apes* (film franchise), United States: 20th Century Fox.

Jenkins, Serena T., Reysen, S., and Katzarska-Miller, Iva. 2012. 'Ingroup Identification and Personality', *Journal of Interpersonal Relations* 5:9–16.

Jenkins, Henry. 1992. *Textual Poachers: Television Fans and Participatory Culture.* London: Routledge.

Jenkins, Henry. 2006. *Convergence Culture: Where Old and New Media Collide*, New York: New York University Press.

Jenner, Mareike. 2016. *American TV Detective Dramas*, Hampshire: Palgrave Macmillan.

Jetten, Jolanda, Spears, Russell, and Manstead, Anthony S. R. 2001. 'Similarity as a Source of Discrimination: The Role of Group Identification', *European Journal of Social Psychology* 31:621–40.

Johnson, Derek. 2007. 'Fan-Tagonism: Factions, Institutions, and Constitutive Hegemonies of Fandom', in *Fandom, Second Edition: Identities and Communities in a Mediated World*, edited by Jonathan Gray, Cornell Sandvoss and C. Lee Harrington, 369–86, New York: New York University Press.

Jones, Meredith. 2017. 'Expressive Surfaces: The Case of the Designer Vagina', *Theory, Culture and Society* 34, 7–8:29–50.

Jordan, Winthrop D. 2012. *White over Black: American Attitudes toward the Negro, 1550-1812*, Chapel Hill: University of North Carolina Press.

Kipnis, Laura. 2006. 'How to Look at Pornography', in *Pornography: Film and Culture (How to Look at Pornography)*, edited by Peter Lehman, 118–29, New Brunswick, NJ: Rutgers University Press.

Kozinets, Robert. 2010. *Netnography: Doing Ethnographic Research Online*, London: Sage Publications.

Lamb, Patricia Frazer, and Veith, Diana L. 2014. 'Romantic Myth, Transcendence, and Star Trek Zines', in *The Fan Fiction Studies Reader*, edited by Karen Hellekson and Kristina Busse, 97–115, Iowa City, IA: University of Iowa Press.

Lambert, Gregg. 2017. 'Meditation on the Animal and the Work of Art', in *Deleuze and the Animal*, edited by Colin Gardner and Patricia MacCormack, 255–65, Edinburgh: Edinburgh University Press.

Lawrence, Anne A. 2009. 'Erotic Target Location Errors: An Underappreciated Paraphilic Dimension', *Journal of Sex Research* 46, 2–3:194–215.

Lay, Samantha. 2007. 'Audiences across the Divide: Game to Film Adaptation and the Case of Resident Evil', *Participations: Journal of Audience and Reception Studies* 4, 2:n.p.

Leavitt, Alex, and Horbinski, Andrea. 2012. 'Even a Monkey Can Understand Fan Activism: Political Speech, Artistic Expression, and a Public for the Japanese Dôjin Community', *Transformative Works and Cultures* 10:n.p.

Levant, Brian. 1992. *Beethoven* (film), United States: Universal Studios.

Levi-Strauss, Claude. 1976. *Structural Anthropology 2*, New York: Penguin Books.

Levi-Strauss, Claude. 1978. *Myth and Meaning*, London: Routledge.

Linehan, Graham. 2006–13. *The I.T. Crowd* (television series), UK: Channel 4.

Live Journal. 2003. 'CSI: As if Furry Cons Could Afford Las Vegas – The Online Computery Journal Thingy of a Turtle', LiveJournal, 30 October 2003. https://kinkyturtle.livejournal.com/92527.html.

Locke, Simon. 2012. 'Fanboy as a Revolutionary Category', *Participations: Journal of Audience and Reception Studies* 9, 2:835–54.

Long, Janet H., and Chen, Guoming. 2007. 'The Impact of Internet Usage on Adolescent Self-Identity Development', *China Media Research* 3, 1:99–109.

Lorre, Chuck. 2007–19. *The Big Bang Theory* (television series), United States: CBS.

MacCormack, Patricia. 2009. 'Queer Posthumanism: Cyborgs, Animals, Monsters, Perverts', in *The Ashgate Research Companion to Queer Theory*, edited by Noreen Giffney and Michael O'Rourke, 111–28, Farnham, UK: Ashgate.

MacCormack, Patricia. 2014. 'Introduction', in *Deleuze and the Animal*, edited by Colin Gardner and Patricia MacCormack, 1–13, Edinburgh: Edinburgh University Press.

MacCormack, Patricia. 2020. *The Ahuman Manifesto: Activism for the End of the Anthropocene*, London: Bloomsbury.

Maher, John T. 2014. 'Legal Technology Confronts Speciesism, or We Have Met the Enemy and He Is Us', in *The Animal Catalyst: Towards Ahuman Theory*, edited by Patricia MacCormack, 27–48, London: Bloomsbury.

Major, Brenda, Kaiser, Cheryl R., and McCoy, Shannon. 2003. 'It's Not My Fault: When and Why Attributions to Prejudice Protect Self-Esteem', *Personality and Social Psychology Bulletin* 29, 6:772–81.

Marsh, Jackie. 2005. 'Ritual, Performance and Identity Construction: Young Children's Engagement with Popular Cultural and Media Texts', in *Popular Culture, New Media and Digital Literacy in Early Childhood*, edited by Jackie Marsh, 28–50, Oxon, UK: Routledge.

Marshall, Catherine, and Rossman, Gretchen B. 2011. *Designing Qualitative Research*, Los Angeles, CA: Sage.

Marx, Karl. 2003. 'On the Jewish Question', in *Identities: Race, Class, Gender and Nationality*, edited by Linda Martin Alcoff and Eduardo Mendieta, 17–28, London: Blackwell.

Massanari, Adrienne Lynne. 2015a. *Participatory Culture, Community and Play: Learning from Reddit*, Bern: Peter Lang.

Massanari, Adrienne Lynne. 2015b. '#Gamergate and the Fappening: How Reddit's Algorithm, Governance, and Culture Support Toxic Technocultures', *New Media and Society* 19, 3:320–46.

Mays, Vicky M., and Cochran, Susan D. 2001. 'Sexual Orientation and Mortality among US Men Aged 17 to 59 Years: Results from the National Health and Nutrition Examination Survey III', *American Journal of Public Health* 101, 6:1133–8.

McCloud, Scott. 1993. *Understanding Comics: The Invisible Art*, New York: William Morrow Paperbacks.

McCrae, Robert R., and Costa, Paul T. 1999. 'A Five-Factor Theory of Personality', in *Handbook of Personality: Theory and Research*, edited by Oliver P. John, Lawrence A. Pervin and Richard W. Robins, 159–81, New York: Guilford Press.

McCracken, Grant. 2008. *Transformations: Identity Construction in Contemporary Culture*, Bloomington: Indiana University Press.

McCudden, Michelle L. 2011. *Degrees of Fandom: Authenticity and Hierarchy in the Age of Media Convergence*, Lawrence: University of Kansas.

McGlotten, Shani. 2014. 'Zombie Porn: Necropolitics, Sex, and Queer Socialities', *Porn Studies* 1, 4:360–77.

McKee. Alan. 2018. 'Porn Consumers as Fans', in *A Companion to Media Fandom and Fan Studies*, edited by Paul Booth, 509–21. New York: Wiley Blackwell.

McMahon, Tom. 2008–12. *1,000 Ways to Die* (television series), United States: Spike.

McNicholas, Suzanne Lamb. 2002. 'Social Support and Positive Health Practices', *Western Journal of Nursing Research* 24:772–87.

Mead, Herbert. 2003. 'The Self', in *Identities: Race, Class, Gender and Nationality*, edited by Linda Martin Alcoff and Eduardo Mendieta, 32–40, London: Blackwell.

Meyer, Stephanie. 2005. *Twilight*, Boston: Little, Brown.

Milner, Ryan M. 2012. *The World Made Meme: Discourse and Identity in Participatory Media*, Lowrence: University of Kansas.

Mulvey, Laura. 1992. 'Visual Pleasure and Narrative Cinema', in *The Sexual Subject: A Screen Reader in Sexuality*, edited by John Caughie and Annette Kuhn, 22–34, London: Routledge.

NBC News. 2015. *Things Are Looking Up in America's Porn Industry* [online]. https://www.nbcnews.com/business/business-news/ things-are-looking-americas-porn-industry-n289431.

Nead, Lynda. 1993. '"Above the Pulp-Line": The Cultural Significance of Erotic Art', in *Dirty Looks: Women, Pornography, Power*, edited by Pamela Church Gibson and Roma Gibson, 144–55, London: BFI.

Nelson, Noah. 2019. 'Furry Fandom Helps Create Culture of Friendship, Respect', *Daily Barometer*, 4 March 2019. http://www.orangemedianetwork.com/daily_barometer/

furry-fandom-helps-create-culture-of-friendship-respect/article_5d3947b8-3e0e-
11e9-af06-8f1efb4e10d8.html.

Nyareon. 2015. 'The Furry Fandom', in *Furries Among Us: Essays on Furries by the Most Prominent Members of the Fandom*, edited by Thurston Howl, 5–11, Nashville TN: Thurston Howl Publications.

Orwell, George. 1945. *Animal Farm*, London: Halas and Bachelor.

Oztok, Murat. 2016. 'Cultural Ways of Constructing Knowledge: The Roles of Identities in Online Group Discussions', *International Society of the Learning Sciences* 11:157–86.

Pachankis, John. 2007. 'The Psychological Implications of Concealing a Stigma: A Cognitive–Affective–Behavioral Model', *Psychological Bulletin* 133, 2:328–45.

Pande, Rukmini. 2018. 'Who Do You Mean by "Fan?" Decolonizing Media Fandom Identity', in *A Companion to Media Fandom and Fan Studies*, edited by Paul Booth, 319–33, New York: Wiley Blackwell.

Patten, Fred. 2012. 'Retrospective: An Illustrated Chronology of Furry Fandom, 1966–1996', *Flayrah*, 15 July 2012. https://www.flayrah.com/4117/retrospective-illustrated-chronology-furry-fandom-1966-1996.

Patten, Fred. 2015. 'The History of Furry Publishing', in *Furries Among Us: Essays on Furries by the Most Prominent Members of the Fandom*, edited by Thurston Howl, 35–47, Nashville TN: Thurston Howl Publications.

Patten, Fred. 2016. 'CALL FOR INFORMATION: Furry Convention History', *Dog Patch Press*, 11 January 2016. http://dogpatch.press/2016/01/11/furry-con-history/.

Patterson, Zabet. 2004. 'Going On-Line: Consuming Pornography in the Digital Age', in *Porn Studies*, edited by Linda Williams, 104–25, Durham, NC: Duke University Press.

Perrotta, Carlo. 2009. *The Construction of a Common Identity through Online Discourse: A Socio-Cultural Study of a Virtual Community*, Bath, UK: University of Bath.

Phillips, Whitney. 2015. *This Is Why We Can't Have Nice Things: Mapping the Relationship between Online Trolling and Mainstream Culture*, Cambridge, MA: MIT Press.

Pinto, Diego Costa, Reale, Getulio, Segabinazzi, Rodrigo, and Vargas Rossi, Carlos Alberto. 2015. 'Online Identity Construction: How Gamers Redefine Their Identity in Experiential Communities', *Journal of Consumer Behaviour* 14:399–409.

Plante, Courtney N., Reysen, Stephen, Roberts, Sharon E., and Gerbasi, Kathleen C. 2016. *FurScience! A Summary of Five Years of Research from the International Anthropomorphic Research Project*, Ontario, Canada: FurScience.

Plante, Courtney N., Roberts, Shannon E., Snider, Jamie S., Schroy, Catherine, Reysen, Stephen, and Gerbasi, Kathleen C. 2015. '"More Than Skin-Deep": Biological

Essentialism in Response to a Distinctiveness Threat in a Stigmatized Fan Community', *British Journal of Social Psychology* 54:359–70.

Plante, Courtney N., Roberts, Shannon E., Reysen, Stephen, and Gerbasi, Kathleen C. 2014. 'Interaction of Socio-Structural Characteristics Predicts Identity Concealment and Self-Esteem in Stigmatized Minority Group Members', *Curr Psychol* 33, 3:3–19.

Poiani, Aldo. 2010. *Animal Homosexuality: A Biological Perspective*, Cambridge: Cambridge University Press.

Probyn-Rapsey, Fiona. 2011. 'Furries and the Limits of Species Identity Disorder: A Response to Gerbasi et al.', *Society and Animals* 19, 3:294–301.

Proctor, William. 2013. '"Holy Crap, More Star Wars! More Star Wars? What if They're Crap?": Disney, Lucasfilm and Star Wars', *Participations: Journal of Audience and Reception Studies* 10, 1:198–224.

Proctor, William. 2016. 'A New Breed of Fan? Regimes of Truth, One Direction Fans and Representations of Enfreakment', in *Seeing Fans: Representations of Fandom in Media and Popular Culture*, edited by Paul Booth and Lucy Bennett, 67–78, London: Bloomsbury Academic.

Proctor, William. 2017. 'Fear of a #Blackstormtrooper: Hashtag Publics, Canonical Fidelity and the Star Wars Platonic', paper presented at the Fan Studies Network Conference, Huddersfield, UK: Huddersfield University.

Pyer, Michelle, and Campbell, Jackie. 2012. 'Qualitative Researching with Vulnerable Groups', *International Journal of Therapy and Rehabilitation* 19, 6:311–16.

Radovic, Ana, Gmelin, Theresa, Stein, Bradley D., and Miller, Elizabeth. 2017. 'Depressed Adolescents' Positive and Negative Use of Social Media', *Journal of Adolescence* 55:5–15.

Radway, Janice. 1984. *Reading the Romance*, Chapel Hill: University of North Carolina Press.

Reeves, Matt. (Director). 2014. *Dawn of the Planet of the Apes* (film), United States: 20th Century Fox.

Reeves, Matt. (Director). 2017. *War of the Planet of the Apes* (film), United States: 20th Century Fox.

Reynolds, Katherine J., Bizumic, Boris, Subasic, Emina, Turner, John C., Branscombe, Nyla R., Mavor, Ken, and Batalha, Luisa. 2012. 'Social Identity and Personality Processes: Non-Aboriginal Australian Identity and Neuroticism', *European Journal of Social Psychology* 42:252–62.

Reysen, Stephen, Plante, Courtney N., Roberts, Shannon E., and Gerbasi, Kathleen C. 2015a. 'Ingroup Bias and Ingroup Projection in the Furry Fandom', *International Journal of Psychological Studies* 7:49–58.

Reysen, Stephen, Plante, Courtney N., Roberts, Shannon E., and Gerbasi, Kathleen C. 2015b. 'A Social Identity Perspective of Personality Differences between Fan and Non-Fan Identities', *World Journal of Social Science Research* 2, 1:91–103.

Reysen, Stephen, Plante, Courtney N., Roberts, Shannon E., and Gerbasi, Kathleen C. 2016. 'Optimal Distinctiveness and Identification with the Furry Fandom', *Curr Psychol* 35:638–42.

Rheingold, Howard. 1993. *Virtual Community: Homesteading on the Electronic Frontier*, Boston: Addison-Wesley.

Rheingold, Howard. 1994. *The Virtual Community*, London: Martin Seeker and Warburg.

Ridings, Catherine M., and Gefen, David. 2004. 'Virtual Community Attraction: Why People Hang Out Online', *Journal of Computer-Mediated Communication* 10, 1:n.p.

Ridout, Brad, Campbell, Andrew, and Ellis, Louise. 2012. '"Off Your Face(Book)": Alcohol in Online Social Identity Construction and Its Relation to Problem Drinking in University Students', *Drug and Alcohol Review* 31:20–6.

Roberts, Shannon E., Plante, Courtney N., Gerbasi, Kathleen C., and Reysen, Stephen. 2015a. 'The Anthrozoomorphic Identity: Furry Fandom Members' Connections to Nonhuman Animals', *Anthrozoös* 28:533–48.

Roberts, Shannon E., Plante, Courtney N., Gerbasi, Kathleen C., and Reysen, Stephen. 2015b. 'Clinical Interaction with Anthropomorphic Phenomenon: Notes for Health Professionals about Interacting with Clients Who Possess This Unusual Identity', *Health and Social Work* 40, 3:42–50.

Robertson, Venetia Laura Delano. 2012. 'The Law of the Jungle: Self and Community in the Online Therianthropy Movement', *Pomegranate: The International Journal of Pagan Studies* 14, 2:256–80.

Rudwick, Stephanie, and Ntuli, Mduduzi. 2009. 'IsiNgqumo: Introducing a Gay Black South African Linguistic Variety', *Southern African Linguistics and Applied Language Studies* 26, 4:445–56.

Russ, Joanna. 2014. 'Pornography by Women for Women, with Love', in *The Fan Fiction Studies Reader*, edited by Karen Hellekson and Kristina Busse, 82–95, Iowa City: University of Iowa Press.

Saldana, Johnny. 2016. *The Coding Manual for Qualitative Researchers*, London: Sage Publications.

Sampasa-Kanyinga, Hugues, and Lewis, Rosamund F. 2015. 'Frequent Use of Social Networking Sites Is Associated with Poor Psychological Functioning Among Children and Adolescents'. *Cyberpsychology Behavior and Social Networking* 18, 7:380–5.

Sandvoss, Cornell. 2011. 'Fans Online: Affective Media Consumption and Production in the Age of Convergence', in *Online Territories: Globalization, Mediated Practice and Social Space*, edited by Miyase Christensen, Andre Jansson and Christian Christensen, 49–74, New York: Peter Lang.

Satinsky, Emily, and Green, Denise Nicole. 2016. 'Negotiating Identities in the Furry Fandom through Costuming', *Critical Studies in Men's Fashion* 3, 2:107–23.

Scodari, Christine. 2007. 'Yoko in Cyberspace with Beatles Fans: Gender and the Re-Creation of Popular Mythology', in *Fandom, Second Edition: Identities and Communities in a Mediated World*, edited by Jonathan Gray, Cornell Sandvoss and C. Lee Harrington, 48–59, New York: New York University Press.

Scott, Suzanne. 2009. Repackaging Fan Culture: The Regifting Economy of Ancillary Content Models, *Transformative Works and Cultures*, 3:n.p.

Scott, Suzanne. 2011. *Revenge of the Fanboy: Convergence Culture and the Politics of Incorporation*, Berkeley: University of California.

Scott, Suzanne. 2012. 'Fangirls in Refrigerators: The Politics of (In)visibility in Comic Book Culture', in Appropriating, Interpreting, and Transforming Comic Books, edited by Matthew J. Costello, special issue, *Transformative Works and Cultures*, 13:n.p.

Sedgwick, Eve. 2003. *Touching, Feeling: Affect, Pedagogy, Performativity*, Durham, NC: Duke University Press.

Segal, Lynne. 1993. 'Does Pornography Cause Violence?: The Search for Evidence', in *Dirty Looks: Women, Pornography, Power*, edited by Pamela Church Gibson and Roma Gibson, 5–22, London: BFI.

Shakespeare, William. 1595–96. *A Midsummer Night's Dream* (theatrical play), London: Globe.

Shamoon, Deborah. 2004. 'Office Sluts and Rebel Flowers: The Pleasures of Japanese Pornographic Comics for Women', in *Porn Studies*, edited by Linda Williams, 90–120, Durham, NC: Duke University Press.

Shifman, Limor. 2014. *Memes in Digital Culture*, Cambridge: MIT Press.

Shoji. 2015. 'Social Furs: An Inside Look at How the Furry Fandom Socializes', in *Furries Among Us: Essays on Furries by the Most Prominent Members of the Fandom*, edited by Thurston Howl, 12–17, Nashville, TN: Thurston Howl Publications.

Shwartz, Josh, and Fedak, Chris. 2007–12. *Chuck* (television series), United States: NBC.

Sidanius, Jim, and Pratto, Felicia, 2001. *Social Dominance: An Intergroup Theory of Social Hierarchy and Oppression*, New York: Cambridge University Press.

Silah, Sara. 2007. 'Filling Up the Space between Mankind and Ape: Racism, Speciesism and the Androphilic Ape', *ARIEL: A Review of International English Literature* 38, 1:95–111.

Smelser, Neil. 2004. 'Psychological Trauma and Cultural Trauma', in *Cultural Trauma and Collective Identity*, edited by Jeffery C. Alexander, Ron Eyerman, Bernhard Giesen, Neil J. Smelser and Piotr Sztompka, 31–59, Berkeley: University of California Press.

Smith, Charles. M. 1997. *Air Bud* (film), USA/Canada: Buena Vista Pictures Distributions Inc./Warner Bros. Pictures.

Soh, Debra W., and Cantor, James M. 2015. 'A Peek Inside a Furry Convention', *Archive of Sexual Behaviour* 44:1–2.

Son Hing, Leanne, 2012. 'Responses to Stigmatization: The Moderating Roles of Primary and Secondary Appraisals', *Du Bois Review* 9, 1:149–68.

Spears, Russell, Doosje, E. J., and Ellemers, Naomi. 1997. 'Self-Stereotyping in the Face of Threats to Group Status and Distinctiveness: The Role of Group Identification', *Personality and Social Psychology Bulletin* 23:538–53.

Spencer, Steven J., Steele, Claude M., and Quinn, Diane M. 1999. 'Stereotype Threat and Women's Math Performance', *Journal of Experimental Social Psychology* 35, 1:4–28.

Springer, Claudia. 1996. *Electronic Eros: Bodies and Desire in the Postindustrial Age*, Austin: University of Texas Press.

Stanfill, Mel. 2011. 'Doing Fandom, (Mis)doing Whiteness: Heteronormativity, Racialization, and the Discursive Construction of Fandom', *Transformative Works and Cultures* 8:n.p.

Stanfill, Mel. 2013a. '"They're Losers, but I Know Better": Intra-Fandom Stereotyping and the Normalization of the Fan Subject', *Critical Studies in Media Communication* 30, 2:117–34.

Stanfill, Mel. 2013b. 'Fandom, Public, Commons', *Transformative Work and Cultures* 14:n.p.

Stanfill, Mel. 2018. 'The Unbearable Whiteness of Fandom and Fan Studies', *A Companion to Media Fandom and Fan Studies*, edited by Paul Booth, 305–18. New York: Wiley Blackwell.

Stanfill, Mel, and Condis, Megan. 2014. 'Fandom and/as Labor', *Transformative Works and Cultures* 15:n.p.

Steele, Claude M., and Aronson, Joshua M. 1995. 'Stereotype Threat and the Intellectual Test Performance of African Americans', *Journal of Personality and Social Psychology* 69, 5:797–811.

Stivale, Charles J. 2014. 'Etre aux aguets: Deleuze, Creation and Territorialisation', in *The Animal Catalyst: Towards Ahuman Theory*, edited by Patricia MacCormack, 69–81, London: Bloomsbury.

Straub, Jurgen. 2002. 'Personal and Collective Identity: A Conceptual Analysis', in *Identities: Time, Difference and Boundaries*, edited by Heidrun Friese, 56–76, Germany: Berghahn Books.

Strike, Joe. 2017. *Furry Nation: The True Story of America's Most Misunderstood Subculture*. Minneapolis, MN: Cleis Press.

Sugar, Rebecca. 2013–19. *Steven Universe* (TV series), United States: Cartoon Network.

Sturken, Marita, and Cartwright, Lisa. 2009. *Practices of Looking: An Introduction to Visual Culture*, Oxford: Oxford University Press.

Tate, Tim. 1990. *Child Pornography: An Investigation*, London: Methuen.

Taylor, Maxwell, and Quayle, Ethel. 2003. *Child Pornography: An Internet Crime*, New York: Brunner-Routledge.

Teague, Lewis. 1983. *Cujo* (film), United States: Warner Bros./PSO International.

Thio, Alex. 2010. *Deviant Behavior*, Boston: Pearson Education.

Thompson, Nato. 2005. 'Introduction', in *Becoming Animal: Contemporary Art in the Animal Kingdom*, edited by Nato Thompson and Christoph Cox, 1–13, North Adams, MA: Mass MoCA Publications.

Toffoletti, Kim. 2007. *Cyborgs and Barbie Dolls: Feminism, Popular Culture and the Posthuman Body*, New York: I.B. Tauris.

Turner, John C., and Onorato, Rina S. 1999. 'Social Identity, Personality, and the Self-Concept: A Self-Categorizing Perspective', in *The Psychology of the Social Self*, edited Tom R. Tyler, Roderick M. Kramer and Oliver P. John, 11–46. Mahwah, NJ: Lawrence Erlbaum Associates.

Van de Goor, Sophie Charlotte. 2015. '"You Must Be New Here": Reinforcing the Good Fan', *Participations: Journal of Audience and Reception Studies* 12, 2:275–95.

Vannini, Phillip, and Franzese, Alexis. 2008. 'The Authenticity of Self: Conceptualization, Personal Experience, and Practice', *Sociology Compass* 2, 5:1621–37.

Vigne, Jean-Denis, Evin, Allowen, Cucchi, Thomas, Dai, Lingling, Yu, Chong, Hu, Songmei, Soulages, Nicolas, Wang, Weilin, Sun, Zhouyong, Gao, Jiangtao, Dobney, Keith, and Yuan, Jing. 2016. 'Earliest "Domestic" Cats in China Identified as Leopard Cat (*Prionailurus bengalensis*)', *PLoS ONE* 11, 1:1–11.

Vygotsky, Lee. 1978. 'Interaction between Learning and Development', in *Readings on the Development of Children*, edited by Mary Gauvain and Michael Cole, 34–40, New York: Scientific American Books.

Wagner, Peter. 2002. 'Identity and Selfhood as Problematique', in *Identities: Time, Difference and Boundaries*, edited by Heidrun Friese, 32–55, Germany: Berghahn Books.

Wann, Daniel, and Branscombe, Nyla R. 1993. 'Sports Fans: Measuring Degree of Identification with Their Team', *International Journal of Sport Psychology* 24:1–17.

Welton, Simon Shires, 2016. *World of Weird* (television documentary), UK: Channel 4.

Whiteman, Natasha, and Metivier, Joanne. 2013. 'From Post-Object to "Zombie" Fandoms: The "Deaths" of Online Fan Communities and What They Say about Us', *Participations: Journal of Audience and Reception Studies* 10, 1:270–98.

WikiFur. 2016. 'RainFurrest' 2016, *WikiFur*, January 2020. https://en.wikifur.com/wiki/RainFurrest_2016.

WikiFur. 2017. 'Fur and Loathing', *WikiFur*, 2017. http://en.wikifur.com/wiki/Fur_and_Loathing.

Wilkins, Abbie M., McCrae, Lucy S., and McBride, E. Anne. 2015. 'Factors Affecting the Human Attribution of Emotions toward Animals', *Anthrozoös* 28, 3:357–69.

Williams, Rebecca. 2015. *Post-Object Fandom: Television, Identity and Self-Narrative*, UK: Bloomsbury.

Williams, Linda. 2004. 'Porn Studies: Proliferating Pornographies, On/Scene: An Introduction', in *Porn Studies*, edited by Linda Williams, 1–24, Durham, NC: Duke University Press.

Williams, David R., Neighbors, Harold W., and Jackson, James S. 2003. Racial/Ethnic Discrimination and Health: Findings from Community Studies. *American Journal of Public Health* 93: 200–8.

Willson, Michele A. 2006. *Technically Together: Rethinking Community with Techno-Society*, New York: Peter Lang.

Wilson, Melody. 2012. 'Brony Love: Lauren Faust, Creator of My Little Pony: Friendship Is Magic, Live from Brony Con', *Bitch Media*, 3 July 2012. https://www.bitchmedia.org/post/lauren-faust-creator-of-my-little-pony-friendship-is-magic-live-from-bronycon-feminist-magazine-bronies-gender-fandom.

Winterman, Denise. 2009. 'Who Are the Furries?', *BBC News*, 13 November 2009. http://news.bbc.co.uk/1/hi/magazine/8355287.stm.

Wittig, Monique. 2006. 'One Is Not Born a Woman', in *Identities: Race, Class, Gender and Nationality*, edited by Linda Martin Alcoff and Eduardo Mendieta, 158–62, London: Blackwell.

Wolfe, Carey. 2010. *What Is Posthumanism?*, Minneapolis: University of Minnesota Press.

Wyatt. Rupert. 2011. *Rise of the Planet of the Apes* (film), United States: 20th Century Fox.

Zuiker, Anthony. E. 2000–15. *CSI: Crime Scene Investigation* (television series), United States: CBS.

Bibliography

Index